Journal of Education for Students Placed At Risk

SPECIAL ISSUE
Where Are They Now?
A Tenth-Anniversary Retrospective

JOURNAL OF EDUCATION FOR STUDENTS PLACED AT RISK, *10*(2), 149–155

Editors' Introduction: Where Are They Now? A Tenth-Anniversary Retrospective

Samuel C. Stringfield
Kirsten Ewart Sundell
College of Education and Human Development
University of Louisville

This volume marks the 10th anniversary of the *Journal of Education for Students Placed At Risk* (*JESPAR*). Our first issue, published in January 1996, introduced our readers to the guiding principles that would define the journal's mission and course over the years that followed. These were the beliefs that (a) schools can have a strong, positive impact on the education of at-risk children, and (b) effective programs exist or can be developed that can improve the educational experiences of at-risk students (Stringfield & Hollifield, 1996). *JESPAR*'s purpose, as stated in the first Editors' Introduction, was to

> offer articles geared to academic researchers, policy analysts, and especially to practitioners regarding practical, research-based progress in the field of education for students placed at risk. The journal will offer refereed research articles on promising programs, descriptions of promising programs in the field, case studies of "schools that work," and research literature reviews. We will stress programs and practices that are practical, are in place, and have been shown through rigorous research to be working. *JESPAR* will focus on programs and practices from which other schools can learn. (Stringfield & Hollifield, 1996, p. 1)

Our mission was derived in part from that of the Center for Research on the Education of Students Placed At Risk (CRESPAR), and the journal was funded by CRESPAR for its first 9 years. Since its founding, the journal has maintained its re-

Requests for reprints should be sent to Kirsten Ewart Sundell, University of Louisville, College of Education and Human Development, ELFH Room 333, Louisville, KY 40292. E-mail: kirsten.sundell@louisville.edu

cord of on-time publication, submitting nearly 40 regular and double issues containing case studies, research papers, book reviews, and commentaries at the forefront of education research. *JESPAR*'s authors have contributed articles on such topics as Title I schoolwide programs; No Child Left Behind; adequate yearly progress; bilingual education; career academies; dropout prevention; Head Start; magnets, vouchers, and charter schools; reform initiatives; school restructuring; urban issues; and comprehensive school reform designs or intervention programs like Success For All, Direct Instruction, Co-Nect, ATLAS, America's Choice, and the Comer School Development Program, among many other subjects. Special issues featured in recent volumes of *JESPAR* have included *When Diversity Works: Bridging Families, Peers, Schools, and Communities at CREDE*; *Direct Instruction Reading Programs: Examining Effectiveness for At-Risk Students in Urban Settings*; *Quest for Quality: An Evaluation of the City–State Partnership in Baltimore's Public Schools*; and *Closing the Achievement Gap*.

JESPAR's slate of regular features has altered somewhat since our first few volumes, but our commitment to reporting on promising, practical programs and timely developments in the field of educating at-risk children has not changed. As part of that commitment, we've dedicated our 10th anniversary year to a series of special issues. Volume 10, Number 1, entitled *Examining the Roles and Possible Roles of State Departments of Education in Comprehensive School Reform* (based on a 2004 AERA panel), was guest edited by Edmund T. Hamann of the Education Alliance at Brown University and appeared in January of 2005. This issue, Volume 10, Number 2, traces the later histories of schools and programs profiled in the earliest issues of *JESPAR*. Volume 10, Number 3, a special issue on data use entitled *Transforming Data into Knowledge: Applications of Data-Based Decision-Making to Improve Educational Practice*, will be guest edited by Jeff Wayman of the Center for Social Organization of Schools at Johns Hopkins University. *The CREDE Synthesis Project: Implications for Research, Policy, and Practice*, guest edited by Roland Tharp of the University of California, Santa Cruz, rounds out Volume 10.

WHERE ARE WE NOW?

Recent developments in national education policy, including No Child Left Behind (2001) and the Education Sciences Reform Act (2002), have increasingly put pressure on education researchers to reevaluate the methods, rigor, focus, and audience for their work. Whitehurst (2003) outlined the mission of the new organization created by the Education Sciences Reform Act, the Institute of Education Sciences, and stressed the need for education research "that has high consideration of use, that is practical, that is applied, that is relevant to practitioners and policy makers." To rise to this challenge, education research must become more data driven; emphasize applied research, randomized field trials, and field-initiated evaluations;

and respond cogently to the consumers of research—teachers, administrators, and other practitioners in the field—with meaningful, scientifically based information on practices and programs that *work*.

What works in schools has always been *JESPAR*'s primary concern. So, too, has been the questions of how change—particularly reform—occurs in schools, why it happens, and what sustains it and makes it flourish. In this issue, articles are presented addressing one of the most vexing issues in school reform: how to sustain, or institutionalize, reforms that have worked. A wide range of long-time observers of school reform efforts have commented on the challenges associated with institutionalizing effective practices (e.g., Cuban & Usdan, 2003; Fullan, 2001). In this issue, we revisit some of the promising programs featured in our earliest issues to see whether what worked for these schools in the past is continuing to work now, as well as to examine how changes in policy and practice have impacted these schools over time. The news is good.

WHERE ARE THEY NOW?

The first issue of *JESPAR* featured a remarkable series of articles on the then-named Hawthorne Elementary School, a well-regarded and nationally publicized Core Knowledge school in San Antonio, Texas. Now known as Hawthorne Academy, the school has undergone a number of significant changes in recent years, including new leadership, the acquisition of charter-school status, the addition of upper grades (the school now accommodates Pre-K through eighth-grade students), and the construction of a new library facility, among other school-site additions.

We saw some of these changes in a visit we made in late September 2004 to Hawthorne Academy and Trinity University, the institution with which Hawthorne continues to enjoy a successful teacher–education program partnership. A day spent with Hawthorne's students, teachers, and administration proved that it is still a "clean, well-lighted place," a home away from home for students and the community at large, and a haven where both academic achievement and personal character are valued and nurtured. Although the hallways are slightly less vibrant than they were 10 years ago, the good news is that Hawthorne's experiment with Core Knowledge has weathered tough times and remains a central focus of the school's academic mission. Hawthorne's students continue to receive a diverse, enriching curriculum: During our visit, classroom activities ranged from readings of Edgar Allan Poe and books on the earliest Americans, to a practical demonstration of batteries and electric power, to a counting and rhyming sing-along that lead to an integrated reading, writing, and coloring exercise for a busy kindergarten class. After school, an ebullient group of seventh graders met in a computer-filled classroom with their teacher sponsor, who supplied them with snacks and soda, to build sophisticated robots out of Lego equipment. The school values the cultural heritage and language of its 84.4% Hispanic student body: Many classrooms are bilingual, and the library has a large collection of Core Knowledge-related Spanish-language texts. Parents regularly stop by the welcoming, sunlight-drenched library to return their children's books and inquire about new acquisitions.

Academically rich and culturally vibrant, Hawthorne is clear proof of what can happen when administrators, teachers, parents, and students make a strong and lasting commitment to learning, community-building, and sustaining reform. Hawthorne benefits from a well-established, unified faculty that includes long-term teachers, Trinity University interns, and a number of new faculty who themselves were once interns at the school. These young teachers are particularly engaged and committed members of the Hawthorne community: Already experienced with Core Knowledge, familiar with the climate and culture of the school, and aware of the expectations placed on them by the state's accountability systems, they are well-placed to guide new interns and assist veteran faculty in charting the school's future while launching their own teaching careers.

"Home"—what it means, how to reach it—is the overarching theme of teachers Debra Mentzer and Tricia Shaughnessy's powerful reflection on Hawthorne's journey on the road to academic success. As in their previous article (1996), Mentzer and Shaughnessy use Dorothy's travels through Oz as a metaphor for Hawthorne's ongoing development from a struggling inner-city Title I elementary school to a thriving Core Knowledge charter school serving Pre-K–8 students. Although Hawthorne's students continue to thrive under the Core Knowledge program, the school has faced considerable obstacles in its path to success over the past decade, including significant leadership changes, brief slumps in both achievement and initiative, increased pressure to conform to state standards and high-stakes testing requirements, and the threatened loss of the Core Knowledge program. Hawthorne's faculty and students have persevered, however. Mentzer and Shaughnessy's article is a valuable reminder from practitioners in the field of what it takes to sustain reform: a community of instructional leaders devoted to continual improvement; faith in the school's students, community, and staff; and willingness to reevaluate continually, acknowledge failures, celebrate successes, and move on when hard times occur.

Bruce M. Frazee, professor of Education at Trinity University and a key participant in its teacher preparation program, wrote the original essay on the University's perspective on Hawthorne (Frazee, 1996). In that article, Frazee outlined how Trinity used the Holmes Group's agenda to create its teacher education program. Hawthorne was one of several schools serving as a practicum and training site for Trinity students. As Frazee first reported, Hawthorne teachers served as mentors to Trinity students and received assistance in their classrooms, and Trinity students gained valuable field experience, academic credits, and confidence in their teaching and classroom management abilities. Collaborating in this article with his daughter, Felicia F. Frazee, currently a student and participant in the teacher preparation program at Trinity, Frazee reflects on the changes that both the Trinity program and Hawthorne have experienced in the past 10 years. Despite significant changes to the program in both administration and content, the partnership between these two schools remains strong and productive.

A decade after the San Antonio Independent School District first evaluated Hawthorne for *JESPAR* (Schubnell, 1996), Elda E. Martinez examines how Hawthorne Academy students—despite increasing standards and assessment pressures from the state—continue to build on the strong gains reported in the 1996 article. Beginning with the year after the initial implementation of Core Knowledge at Hawthorne in 1992–1993, Martinez analyzes 10 years (1994–2004) of student test score data and concludes that, with only a few interruptions and exceptions, Hawthorne students persist in making substantial gains compared to their counterparts in the district as a whole. She believes that "curriculum-sequencing and increased content knowledge development will continue to lead to increased student achievement" at this school.

The subject of Fay E. Brown and Edward T. Murray's article is Davis Street School, originally featured in *JESPAR*, Volume 3, Number 1 (Brown, Maholmes, Murray, & Nathan, 1998). Davis Street is a New Haven, Connecticut elementary school implementing the School Development Program's Essentials of Literacy process. Begun in the 1996–1997 school year as a pilot project at Davis Street, Essentials of Literacy has proven to be a great success not only for the school, but for the district as well, which accepted it as their primary intervention model for struggling readers. Brown and Murray report on the positive gains in reading that continue to be made by Davis Street and New Haven students.

Christine L. Emmons of the Yale University Child Study Center and Ruth Baskerville, principal of Norman S. Weir Elementary in Paterson, New Jersey, report on that school's progress with the Comer School Development Program since the publication of the first essay on Norman S. Weir in *JESPAR*, Volume 3, Number 1 (Emmons, Efimba, & Hagopian, 1998). That article outlined how Norman S. Weir adopted the Comer program in 1991 as part of a school restructuring effort required by the Paterson school district. As a result of this whole-school change, Norman S. Weir went from being one of the lowest performing schools in the district to one of the highest; it is pleasing that, 7 years after the original *JESPAR* article, Emmons and Baskerville are able to report that the majority of Norman S. Weir students continue to achieve advanced or full proficiency on New Jersey assessments, often out-performing their counterparts in the district and state as a whole. Despite changes in leadership and testing requirements, morale, climate, and expectations remain positive and high at this school.

Pamela S. Nesselrodt and Christianna L. Alger's article on Silverstein Elementary[1] revisits an inner-city school using a university-run coaching/tutoring

---

[1]For confidentiality reasons, the name of the school has been changed.

program to assist at-risk seventh and eighth graders with reading and mathematics. This school's experiment with Mortimer Adler's (1984) Paideia program, first begun in 1983, continues to produce positive results. Nesselrodt and Alger's article highlights the advantages Silverstein students receive from receiving tutoring services from university education students.

Two book reviews by Shelley H. Billig and Robert J. Stevens round out the issue. Billig examines *No Child Left Behind? The Politics and Practice of School Accountability*, edited by Paul E. Peterson and Martin R. West, and discusses the rise of the standards movement, the passing of NCLB, and the impacts these developments have had on policy and practice in American schools, many of which are, like the schools described in this issue, struggling to balance their current reform and improvement programs with mounting accountability pressures. Stevens brings us back to the most important educational domain, the classroom, in his review of Jennifer King Rice's *Teacher Quality: Understanding the Effectiveness of Teacher Attributes*. This text, he states, outlines important variables—teacher experience, teacher preparation and degree, teacher certification, teacher coursework, and teacher test scores—of great significance to policy discussions post-NCLB.

As a final note, we need to report on a significant change that the journal itself has experienced. After 9 years at the Center for Social Organization of Schools at Johns Hopkins University, we have moved to a new home in the College of Education and Human Development at the University of Louisville. We thank our past collaborators and colleagues at Johns Hopkins for their invaluable intellectual, financial, and emotional support, and wish them the best in their future research endeavors. We are excited to join the faculty and staff at the University of Louisville, and thank Dean Robert Felner for welcoming *JESPAR* to Louisville. Finally, we thank you, our readers and contributors, for your unstinting support, patronage, and interest over the past decade. We hope you'll join us for our next 10 years.

Samuel C. Stringfield, Editor
Kirsten E. Sundell, Managing Editor
Journal of Education for Students Placed At Risk
College of Education and Human Development
University of Louisville

REFERENCES

Adler, M. J. (1984). *The Paideia program: An educational syllabus*. New York: Macmillan.

Brown, F. E., Maholmes, V., Murray, E., & Nathan, L. (1998). Davis Street Magnet School: Linking child development with literacy. *Journal of Education for Students Placed At Risk, 31*, 23–38.

Cuban, L., & Usdan, M. (2003). *Powerful reforms with shallow roots*. New York: Teachers College Press.

Emmons, C. L., Efimba, M. O., & Hagopian, G. (1998). A school transformed: The case of Norman S. Weir. *Journal of Education for Students Placed At Risk, 3*, 39–51.

Frazee, B. M. (1996). Hawthorne Elementary School: The university perspective. *Journal of Education for Students Placed At Risk, 1*, 25–31.

Fullan, M. (2001). *The new meaning of educational change* (3rd ed.). New York: Teachers College Press.

Mentzer, D., & Shaughnessy, T. (1996). Hawthorne Elementary School: The teachers' perspective. *Journal of Education for Students Placed At Risk, 1*, 13–23.

Schubnell, G. O. (1996). Hawthorne Elementary School: The evaluator's perspective. *Journal of Education for Students Placed At Risk, 1*, 33–40.

Stringfield, S. C., & Hollifield, J. H. (1996). Editors' introduction. *Journal of Education for Students Placed At Risk, 1*, 1–4.

Whitehurst, G. (2003, April). *The Institute of Education Sciences: New wine and new bottles*. Invited presentation at the annual meeting of the American Educational Research Association, Chicago, IL. Retrieved September 30, 2004, from http://www.ed.gov/rschstat/research/pubs/ies.html

JOURNAL OF EDUCATION FOR STUDENTS PLACED AT RISK, *10*(2), 157–164

Hawthorne Academy:
The Teachers' Perspective

Debra Mentzer
Tricia Shaughnessy
Hawthorne Academy
San Antonio, TX

In 1987, Hawthorne Elementary School battled all of the problems common to inner-city schools: low achievement, inconsistent attendance, and a transient population with student behaviors ranging from apathetic to disruptive. We could see that if we did not do something to break the cycle of failure, our students would end up on the streets or dead. Hawthorne and the San Antonio Independent School District entered into a partnership with Trinity University and a Texas Education Agency initiative to reform our school from within. This initial journey was not without its difficulties, but perhaps the most significant—and ultimately the longest lasting—step we took on that journey was our decision to adopt the Core Knowledge Sequence as our school's curriculum.

Our previous article chronicled the beginning of the journey to educational excellence that our students so richly deserved. We initially compared the changes in our school to the tornado that transformed Dorothy's gray world into the multicolored Land of Oz (Mentzer & Shaughnessy, 1996). Our continuing journey to excellence can be compared to Dorothy's quest to go home.

What is home? A place that is secure, stable, and known. Just as Dorothy would never see her home as a drab place, neither do we at our school. However, Hawthorne Academy does not have the glitz and glamour of the fantasy world of Oz. Perhaps the journey to home is as valid a comparison to the journey our school has undergone in its search for success.

Though Core Knowledge is still the program that spurred the tornado of change at Hawthorne, it has been buffered by the realities of educational challenges and expectations. We have weathered those changes and created a home for students and staff

Requests for reprints should be sent to Debra Mentzer and Tricia Shaughnessy, Hawthorne Academy, San Antonio Independent School District, 115 West Josephine Street, San Antonio, TX 78212. E-mail: debramentzer@earthlink.net

that is stable yet flexible, predictable yet enlightened, safe yet constantly striving for growth. Join us as we recount the journey that has not yet been completed.

Home is Hawthorne Academy, now a Pre-K through eighth-grade Core Knowledge internal charter school in the San Antonio Independent School District (SAISD). It is an inner-city Title I school that has strong and consistent test scores and high academic and community respect.

The early transformation of Hawthorne's academic climate was spearheaded by the Trinity Alliance for Better Schools, SAISD, the Core Knowledge Foundation, and a principal who put it all together. Beginning in 1991, principal Maureen Fitzgerald-Gray created an environment for all of the stakeholders to not just be heard but to get involved. The change was magical, hence our comparison of Hawthorne to the Land of Oz. Parents were involved, students were happy, teachers were cooperative, and test scores rose. What could be better? We were riding high and happy.

Then things changed. At the height of our success, both the principal and the SAISD superintendent retired. Two key leaders were no longer there to support and guide us. While this was a concern, the staff, partnerships, community, and our educational beliefs remained; we assumed that things would continue to proceed as positively as they had before.

Little did we understand the impact of the change in leadership; nor did we recognize the power of the growth in standards-based accountability. In this article, we will address these two issues and their influence on the changes that have created the home we call Hawthorne Academy. It is a tale of difficulties, obstacles, perseverance, and the discovery of talents hidden within all of us.

WHAT YELLOW BRICK ROAD?

Much like Dorothy, who relied on the good witch, Glinda, to guide her on, we relied on the leadership of principal Maureen Fitzgerald-Gray. It is well known that the principal is a school's key instructional leader (Sergiovanni, 1990). When Fitzgerald-Gray retired, we were left with a path to follow and a sense of direction, but troubled by a profound sense of insecurity as to what lay ahead.

Alan L. Wilkins (1989) suggested reflecting on a school's history and honoring the past by identifying eras, much as one might do in a history class. This is an excellent way to explain the challenges and changes brought about by administrative personnel.

Hawthorne's first era could be called the Renaissance, an Era of Enlightenment (1991–1995). This was when everything came together. Core Knowledge Foundation, Trinity University, SAISD, staff, students, and parents were all actively engaged and working as a unit to create the excellence described in our 1996 *JESPAR* article. Enthusiasm abounded, new ideas were greeted with open arms, and collegial problem solving was at its best. It would not be exaggerating to say that, as teachers, we relished our successes and saw a boundless future for our school, our students, and ourselves.

The next era could be best described as the Era of Coasting (1995 to December 1997). The new leadership inherited a school that was respected and viewed as "successful." Visitors came from around the nation and from overseas. The principal chose not to make any changes to the existing program. While this sounded wonderful on the surface, the reality was that no changes at all were made. Continual progress was abandoned in favor of the status quo. However, practices, expectations, and staff were changing, and no adjustments were made to our program. The school was coasting on its reputation and its past. Unfortunately, we were no longer leading, since we had not continued improving. We were mired in the middle. Enthusiasm lagged, test scores plateaued, and the sparks of our vision became dull.

A cadre of teachers assumed the mantle of leadership. We saw that we were not growing, and through the site-based team, began looking at where we were and making plans for furthering our vision. Though the mission of the school and the vision that created it were held dear, our collective sense of direction was not clear. We did not gather data to validate our successes or provide insight for adjustments. We proceeded on the basis of our personal and collective beliefs. While this era was not progressive, we at least maintained the level of our early success. The next era would prove to be much more challenging.

The Era of Deletion (January 1998 to May 2000) was marked by much conflict and concern. Leadership wanted us to delete portions of our school structure and vision in order to adapt to and adopt a plan for raising test scores in light of the institution of high-stakes state testing. All areas of the curriculum were on the chopping block. Our Core Knowledge-based curriculum was targeted, as well as instructional institutions such as reading buddies, readers' theater, and students sharing their work in a public format. Because we had not gathered defined data on their efficacy, these programs were at risk. If we could not clearly defend a program, the administration determined that it had to be cleaned out to rebuild.

Decision making became top-down, and as a result, staff involvement was largely symbolic, not authentic. Choices were given, but the range of options presented to staff were restricted. Site-based decision making was reduced to rubber stamping, and little to no discussion was allowed. Again, a cadre of teachers who held the shared vision began to work to prove their beliefs. This led to conflict among the staff and administration as well as in the community at large.

Instructional leadership shifted to the staff. We vowed to persevere, modeling our strategy on the three forms of perseverance found in successful leaders as described by Lindsey, Homes, and McCall, Jr. (1987), Center for Creative Leadership researchers. We held fast to our beliefs, moved ahead with trying to improve our programs and reach our goals, and resolved to survive the tough times, bouncing back after each setback. We discovered our inner talents and became a community of leaders (Barth, 1991).

This perseverance, persistence, and commitment prevailed, however, and the Deletion Era gave way to the Era of Mourning and Moving On (2000–2002). Our new principal, Thelma Celestino, had been a teacher during the Era of Enlightenment and shared the Hawthorne vision and mission. However, she was astute enough to realize that damage had been done. The school's commitment to the Core Knowledge curriculum and strong collaborative spirit had suffered. The school was no longer viewed with respect or as a model of educational improvement and collegiality. She led us through a process of mourning. We celebrated our past successes, grieved our losses, then reflected on what remained of our early vision. As a collective staff, we began the task of identifying how to improve in light of the new reality of district and state mandates.

Relying on our internal instructional leadership, our community of leaders, things began to heal and we identified methods to bridge the new gaps between curriculum and assessment that had appeared. However, the principal was so effective in turning around the school that the district moved her to a central office position. Another era was beginning just as we started to see students' successes grow.

Fortunately, our new principal, Pita Rodriguez-Pollock, was also a member of our staff during the Era of Enlightenment; once again, she shared our vision. She served as an assistant principal during the Era of Mourning and Moving On and was intimately aware of our struggles and our hopes. She could easily continue our process of growth.

This brings us to our current era, the Era of Renewal. We again have found our shared vision and the level of collegiality in the school is growing. We designed a new Hawthorne: The Hawthorne Academy serves our students from the age of 3 through their middle school years. Our curriculum is still based on the Core Knowledge Sequence, but it is tightly aligned with state and district standards. Things are not quite as colorful, but the results are solid and highly successful. Our reputation as a school of high academic expectations and excellence is also being renewed.

FLYING MONKEYS AND OTHER OBSTACLES

Though following the yellow brick road to find our way was difficult, we encountered many other obstacles as well. Just as Dorothy and her cohorts dodged naysayers, false wizards, and flying monkeys, we had to face and overcome other challenges in our journey to find our home called Hawthorne.

How many times have we as educators had to answer this question, "Are you sure that will work?" or "Is this (fill in the blank) program effective for your children?" or "What's going to happen to our test scores?" Sound familiar? These and many other questions have been asked by us and of us as we have taken this journey with our peers and our students. We have realized that our path contains many bumps, and one of the greatest, sometimes perceived as insurmountable, has been high-stakes testing. Simultaneously, we have learned to remain strong in our beliefs; in other words, we have learned to persevere with what we know is good for kids. The Core Knowledge curriculum is good for kids (Mac Iver, Stringfield, & McHugh, 2000; McHugh & Stringfield, 1999; Stringfield, Datnow, Borman, & Rachuba, 2000).

This has not been an easy road. As the state standards have changed, we have had to change. Our campus staff has realigned and correlated the standards, skills, and the curriculum many times. In the beginning, our skills and standards were broad based. For example, in Social Studies, one skill was teaching American heroes. Our question then was, "What heroes?" The Core Knowledge curriculum was essential as it gave us solid, specific knowledge on which to ground our teaching. In addition, we had many areas where the students continued to receive the same knowledge over and over again. An example of this would be dinosaurs. The students in kindergarten and first grade were experts on dinosaurs; however, those same students received the same knowledge about dinosaurs until the fourth or fifth grade. The Core Knowledge curriculum was essential in getting properly sequenced and increasingly challenging knowledge to the students.

Many educators across the country have had similar dilemmas to the ones listed above. Standards and skills have been so general and vague that the Core Knowledge Sequence has been a natural fit. In recent years, however, states have altered their standards and skills to ones that were more specific in nature, and the era of higher accountability for students, teachers, schools, and districts was born. This culture has become so pervasive that testing now drives the curriculum in many places. In most states, the new laws transformed classrooms into test-preparation centers. Students are being coached to pass tests instead of learning a rich curriculum that prepares them for life in the 21st century (Neill, 2003). Once again, we have had to persevere through this change. This has been an ever-evolving process, one we will never finish. We now know that change is the only constant.

Texas was one of the first states to embrace this idea of high educational accountability. It took some time for us to convince all the stakeholders that we could weather this storm. Several times, the Core Knowledge Sequence was almost discarded. Genuine accountability requires that those most involved play a central role in the design (Neill, 2003). Finally, the staff designed and redesigned our curriculum to be driven by state standards *and* use the Core Knowledge Sequence as the vehicle content for the development of these skills and standards. Our community partners helped a great deal in this effort. Money, time, waivers, and brainpower augmented this work.

Funded with support from Trinity University, we met as a complete staff for a week at the end of the 2001–2002 school year to realign the Core Knowledge Sequence with the updated Texas Essential Knowledge and Skills (TEKS). Grade-level teams met and mapped out the instructional plan by organizing the

Core Knowledge Sequence into our four quarters. The larger task was still at hand—the integration of the state standards (TEKS) and testing objectives.

This process involved cutting up the state standards, discipline by discipline, and identifying correlated content from the Core Knowledge Sequence. Grade levels had many items that were not aligned, and decisions had to be made on when and where those items were going to be taught. Content-specific standards provided the most difficulty. For example, the third-grade TEKS state the following:

> **3.11 Science concepts.** The student knows that the natural world includes earth materials and objects in the sky. The student is expected to:
> (B) identify and record properties of soils such as color and texture, capacity to retain water, and ability to support the growth of plants.

However, the fourth grade studies soils in a unit called Geology: The Earth and Its Changes in Rocks and Weathering and Erosion. It was decided that the TEKS would drive the curriculum in our school; hence the content would be taught at both grade levels. The third-grade teachers made a professional decision to teach the aforementioned TEKS component within their Core Knowledge astronomy unit and expanded the content to address these specific TEKS.

In keeping with the philosophy of using the TEKS as our priority, we reformatted our curriculum document, placed the TEKS on the left-hand side and put the Core Knowledge Sequence on the right. This powerful visual device served as a psychological reminder to teachers and administrators of the reality of the state's rigorous standards: The school would address the TEKS first and use the Core Knowledge Sequence as the content that enriches the standards and engages the students. This was a laborious task, but one that has provided us with a seamless integration of the Core Knowledge Sequence and the state standards that will, in tandem, lead to student success.

District, state, and federal requirements, mandates, programs, and curricula have been some of the many challenges we have faced in Hawthorne's curriculum alignment and realignment. Skills and standards are constantly being refined and infused with new vigor. Yet there has been a loss of autonomy in the classroom as to scope and pacing; teaching is prescribed. So, too, is methodology. This has created a continual source of mixed messages for the educator. Many teachers feel that they are being told to "Do Core Knowledge but make sure you satisfy this state or district requirement first." Some teachers and administrators have difficulty handling the competing demands of this message, especially those teachers who are not confident in their instructional abilities and who, as a result, return to concrete, prescribed practices that will produce a known result in the face of high-stakes accountability. Despite these pressures, we are here to tell you that

Core Knowledge *is* good for kids (see the accompanying article on Hawthorne by Elda Martinez in this issue).

Educators have faced a constant balancing act, having to choose between teaching specifically to test objectives or integrating the Core Knowledge Sequence to teach the skill and working on generalizing skills to testing objectives. Given the constraints of time, needs, and expectations, we have had to persevere with what we know is effective for our students. Some recent research reports are the latest in a series of studies that demonstrate that the higher the stakes, the more teachers will teach to the test—often with harmful effects (Clarke et al., 2003; Pedulla et al., 2003). We have had to persevere in our belief that Core Knowledge is the vehicle that provides connections to prior knowledge, which in turn aids in the development and understanding of a new objective, skill, or standard.

As Roland Barth (1991) stated, "All teachers can lead" (p. 123). He went on to state that "every teacher is good, wants to become good, and can become good" (p. 124). At Hawthorne, we would like to revise that statement by making it clear that teachers must believe this about themselves. When we are able to believe and persevere through the complexities and competing interests of educational reform, we can accomplish wonderful things for our students and ourselves.

ARE WE HOME YET?

Dorothy realized that there is no place like home. Though we agree with the sentiment of her epiphany, the reality in education is that home is really a constant quest. The journey to educational improvement is continual. We strive to create the best place for our students, but that work is never truly completed. However, there are lessons that we have learned in our particular journey at Hawthorne.

The most significant of those lessons learned is the benefit of having a community of leaders. This is the cornerstone of our ongoing growth. The commitment to our shared beliefs created a bond between staff members that led to the development of a community of leaders. We have found that the development of a leadership community helps the school and its reform persevere through many changes and challenges. It provides for a source of stability that allows educational reform to make long-term systemic improvement.

To sustain this community of leaders, we must take proactive measures to expand its membership. One of our early failures was the lack of a mentoring plan for new staff members. Mentorship was done informally at some grade levels. This mentorship relied on personal and professional bonding and assistance. We did not have a formal schoolwide plan to share the vision, mission, expectations, or traditions of Hawthorne. Things were told to new staff members, but the philosophy behind why these things were present in our school culture was not necessarily shared. We are currently looking at creating more universal mentoring methods to provide a clearer understanding, not just of what Hawthorne is all about, but why it is the place it is.

The team that escorted Dorothy through Oz discovered their unique talents and persevered through their obstacles, trials, and tribulations to see her safely home. Our cadre of staff, our internal instructional leadership, have persevered and helped escort Hawthorne toward home. We, too, have weathered many challenges but relied on our group and their talents to create a haven for students and staff that is stable yet flexible, predictable yet enlightened, safe yet constantly striving to reach new heights of excellence and achievement.

REFERENCES

Barth, R. S. (1991). *Improving schools from within.* San Francisco: Jossey-Bass.

Clarke, M., Shore, A., Rhoades, K., Abrams, L., Miao, J., & Li, J. (2003, January). *Perceived effects of state-mandated testing programs on teaching and learning: Findings from interviews with educators in low-, medium-, and high-stakes states.* Boston: National Board on Educational Testing and Public Policy, Boston College. Retrieved August 21, 2004, from http://www.bc.edu/research/nbetpp/statements/nbr1.pdf

Lindsey, E. H., Homes, V., & McCall, M. W., Jr. (1987). *Key events in executives' lives* (Technical Report No. 32). Greensboro, NC: Center for Creative Leadership.

Mac Iver, M. A., Stringfield, S., & McHugh, B. (2000). *Core Knowledge Curriculum: Five-year analysis of implementation and effects in five Maryland schools* (Report No. 50). Baltimore: Center for Research on the Education of Students Placed At Risk, Johns Hopkins University. Retrieved August 21, 2004, from http://www.csos.jhu.edu/crespar/techReports/Report50.pdf

McHugh, B., & Stringfield, S. (1999). Core Knowledge Curriculum: Three-year analysis of implementation and effects in five schools (Report No. 40). Baltimore: Center for Research on the Education of Students Placed At Risk, Johns Hopkins University. Retrieved August 21, 2004, from http://www.csos.jhu.edu/crespar/techReports/Report40.pdf

Mentzer, D., & Shaughnessy, T. (1996). Hawthorne Elementary School: The teachers' perspective. *Journal of Education for Students Placed At Risk, 1,* 13–23.

Neill, M. (2003, November). Leaving children behind: How No Child Left Behind will fail our children. *Phi Delta Kappan, 85,* 225–228. Retrieved August 21, 2004, from http://www.fairtest.org/nattest/Kappan.pdf

Pedulla, J. J., Abrams, L. M., Madaus, G. F., Russell, M. K., Ramos, M. A., & Miao, J. (2003, March). *Perceived effects of state-mandated testing programs on teaching and learning: Findings from a national survey of teachers.* Boston: National Board on Educational Testing and Public Policy, Boston College. Retrieved August 21, 2004, from http://www.bc.edu/research/nbetpp/statements/nbr2.pdf

Sergiovanni, T. J. (1990). *Value-added leadership: How to get extraordinary performance in schools.* San Diego: Harcourt Brace Jovanovich.

Stringfield, S., Datnow, A., Borman, G., & Rachuba, L. (2000). *National evaluation of Core Knowledge Sequence implementation: Final report* (Report No. 49). Baltimore: Center for Research on the Education of Students Placed At Risk, Johns Hopkins University. Retrieved August 21, 2004, from http://www.csos.jhu.edu/crespar/techReports/Report49.pdf

Wilkins, A. L. (1989). *Developing corporate character.* San Francisco: Jossey-Bass.

JOURNAL OF EDUCATION FOR STUDENTS PLACED AT RISK, *10*(2), 165–172

Hawthorne Academy:
The University Perspective

Bruce M. Frazee and Felicia F. Frazee
Department of Education
Trinity University

This article revisits the Trinity University and Hawthorne School partnership since the first case study written 10 years ago. This new perspective analyzes the teacher education program—particularly beliefs and attitudes about it and changes made to the program—with an eye to two primary themes: preparing future teachers and Hawthorne's Core Knowledge curriculum. To gain a varied insight, the second author, Felicia Frazee, a current Trinity teacher education candidate, surveyed and interviewed Hawthorne teachers. Ten years ago, Felicia and I visited Hawthorne together; next year, she plans to be an intern at Hawthorne. To better understand our latest visit, we provide a brief summary of the original essay, *Hawthorne Elementary School: The University Perspective* (Frazee, 1996), to compare the previous program description to the current program description discussed here.

SUMMARY OF THE PAST TEACHER EDUCATION
PROGRAM AT TRINITY

Trinity University was a charter member of the Holmes Group. The initial national agenda of Holmes was to make teacher education more rigorous by creating standards and conditions for universities and schools to work together (Holmes, 1986). Holmes (1990) expanded its goals to promote learning communities for all students while promoting professional development schools as a new institution. The Holmes agenda served as a blueprint for Trinity University to organize its teacher education program. Many teachers from a variety of districts in San Antonio, Texas, participated in forums to produce a model for a new 5-year Master of Arts in

---

Requests for reprints should be sent to Bruce M. Frazee, Department of Education, Trinity University, 1 Trinity Place, San Antonio, TX 78212–7200. Email: bfrazee@trinity.edu

Teaching program. It was from these conversations that local teachers, administrators, and Trinity University professors developed guidelines, roles, and responsibilities for the professional development schools. A Hawthorne teacher described her experience in an article in the Wall Street Journal: "There's been lots of reports telling me what is wrong with education, but for the first time someone [Trinity University] has had enough faith in me as a professional to prescribe a cure" (Putka, 1991). Students in the initial program enrolled as humanities majors for 4 years. There was and is no major in education, until the MAT (Master of Arts in Teaching) in the 5th year. However, students enrolled in 18 hr of education courses with an emphasis on practicum courses in the professional development schools. Koppich (2000) noted that undergraduate students enrolled in a minimum of 135 hr in a professional development school.

Hawthorne is located in the San Antonio Independent School District, situated in a poor industrial area of the city. Most Hawthorne students are bused from other neighborhoods, live in rental apartments, and move frequently. Hawthorne became a Core Knowledge school in 1992. The Core Knowledge curriculum gave these disadvantaged students critical background knowledge. According to a study by Koppich (2000), Hawthorne was

> a constant buzz of activity and a demonstration that children from classically disadvantaged backgrounds, whose own parents have little education, can thrive in an academically challenging environment. What contributes to the success of Hawthorne, according to its faculty, is the integration of content knowledge and skill development. Students practice skills in the context of engaging curriculum. (pp. 13–14)

CURRENT 5-YEAR TEACHER EDUCATION PROGRAM

As part of its teacher preparation program, Trinity still offers its undergraduates who are preparing to teach at the elementary school level a thorough 4-year course of study in the humanities. A Trinity humanities major incorporates revised education courses with different and fewer hours of field-based experience at Hawthorne. The school-based practicum courses now meet more regularly at the university instead of at the professional development school sites. Students are also required to enroll in a practicum class at the middle or high school level, again with less emphasis on time spent in the schools. There were also many changes in the academic foundations courses at the undergraduate level due to certification and standards requirements.

In the 5th year of the program, after completing the Bachelor of Arts degree, course work and assignments still provide a school-based 1-year teaching internship combined with a supportive mentor teacher and a university professor. The students, or "interns," still begin their graduate 5th-year teacher education program with 6 graduate hours of summer classes. Before school starts, the interns attend school staff development sessions with their mentor teachers. Studies at Trinity continue with a pedagogy class that meets one evening each week at the university and a seminar class at the school or university. Interns also must complete a diverse learners class in the fall and a school leadership class in the spring. At the end of the academic year, students deliver a roundtable presentation to parents and mentors to articulate their personal learning and teaching beliefs. Interns who complete all requirements and an electronic portfolio earn a Master of Arts degree in teaching with the appropriate teaching certificates when they pass the Texas certification exams. Some interns take extra state tests to be certified in areas such as special education or bilingual education.

The professional development schools for each certification level continue to meet to form a larger group called the Advisory Council. These exemplar partner schools and the mentors who work with the interns at all grade levels assume a vital role in the management and quality of the teacher education program. The Advisory Council meets several times a year with the university education faculty to discuss the program and the school improvement projects related to each school. Currently, the Advisory Council is not as active as was stated in the initial case study (Frazee, 1996) due to changes in leadership and other program changes, as we describe later.

A key factor in the long-term success of Trinity's teacher education program is the ability of the university education professors to work cooperatively in the professional development schools while also maintaining university responsibilities. Teacher educators must promote good teaching and assist student teachers (interns) in learning from a wide variety of experiences (Johnston, 1994). For this to be possible, the mentor teacher and the university professor must frequently meet, communicate, and reflect with the interns and each other. Additionally, the university professor must develop trusting relationships with the principal, mentor teachers, parents, school staff, and interns to create a successful learning community. The interns receive intensive real-life training at Hawthorne, and the mentors learn and expand their pedagogy through research, organizational support, and staff development provided by the combined efforts of the partnership. Part of the university commitment to Hawthorne is to provide professional development and funding for a school reform model. Hawthorne selected and continues to use Core Knowledge as its reform model.

CORE KNOWLEDGE SEQUENCE CONTINUES AS A REFORM MODEL

The Core Knowledge Sequence: Content Guidelines for Grades K–6 (Core Knowledge Foundation, 2001) provides a solid, shared, specific, and sequenced content guide to build a foundation of knowledge that students need to apply skills. Teachers at Hawthorne are committed to this curriculum because of its positive impact on student learning (see Table 1). Hawthorne teachers know that solid knowledge helps students make meaningful connections between content, skills, and new knowledge. The Core Knowledge Sequence helps reduce redundancy and repetitions; it also helps to integrate and organize content in a motivating way for students. Hawthorne teachers know that facts and skills cannot be taught in isolation and that to use higher order thinking skills, students must enter the classroom with a solid knowledge base. Educators who view Core Knowledge as "rote learning of isolated facts are simply misinformed or have too little faith in teachers" (Frazee, 1993, p. 28).

Teachers and interns plan lessons using this specific content, and Hawthorne teachers, mentors, and interns plan and write Core Knowledge units. Many mentors and interns over the years have presented their units at the Core Knowledge Annual Meeting. Several teachers are mentors and consultants for schools across the country. The partnership between Hawthorne and Trinity is strengthened with Core Knowledge because it provides a focus for all participants in the Hawthorne community. The university, school, administrators, interns, mentors, and parents all know what content is taught at Hawthorne. The Core Knowledge Sequence has been a useful and successful curriculum reform model and has maintained its relevance since the initial case study. However, change has occurred in two other areas: leadership and national and state reforms. These two areas have created program changes at both Trinity University and Hawthorne over the last 10 years.

LEADERSHIP AND REFORM CHANGES

Leadership is an important ingredient for a successful partnership. A new university president and district superintendent both agreed to continue to support the partnership agreement. Without their support, it could not be sustained. In addition, the education department chairperson at Trinity has changed; over the course of 10 years, Hawthorne has had three principals. These new leaders brought change because each leader wanted to establish and develop new programs that reflected their leadership; new leaders often do not choose to maintain the status quo or continue existing programs developed by their predecessors. This is particularly true at Hawthorne, where one of the principals sought, applied for, and was granted in-district charter school status. As part of the charter, preschool (3-, 4-, and 5-year-olds) and middle grades (sixth, seventh, and eighth grades) are gradually being added to the school; this process will be completed by the 2004–2005 school year. A district bond issue passed that allowed for added classrooms and a new library in 2002. Also, the Texas Education Agency devised new standards and expectations for student performance. These changes in standards required an alignment of the Core Knowledge Sequence to the new standards to ensure that the Hawthorne students were meeting state and district expectations. Throughout all these changes, the Core Knowledge Sequence maintained its importance as part of the charter largely because it is designed and sequenced to meet preschool to Grade 8 content.

Trinity's new chairperson also envisioned a change in the restructuring of the 5-year teacher education program because the Texas Education Agency (TEA) changed the state certification level from elementary (Grades 1–6) to early childhood/elementary (3-, 4-, and 5-year-olds to Grade 4). Most of these changes were coursework additions to satisfy the TEA. These course changes were attached to teacher education reform standards, which in turn helped to move the revisions through the university committees and councils. Several of the humanities courses were changed or added to the program to satisfy content expectations of the TEA. The 1-hour practicum courses in the old program gave undergraduates interested in education the opportunity to spend time in a variety of school settings. These courses are now professor-controlled courses instead of mentor-controlled courses; they now meet in only a few select classrooms at Hawthorne. This course change has a direct impact on the hours that students could freely use to develop relationships and seek classroom experiences with a variety of mentors. The new practicum classes increase hours at the university and extol theory over practice in the professional development school. In addition, these revised practicums require one of the course experiences to be at a certification level other than early childhood/elementary. Starting this year, students will also be required to enroll in four special education classes. The hour requirements for the program increased and are becoming highly prescribed. These changes lessen the amount of time that students spend at Hawthorne. Oddly, especially compared to my previous case study for *JESPAR* (1996), there was little if any involvement from the partner schools as these changes were discussed and developed.

TEACHER SURVEY RESULTS

A survey was administered to all of the Hawthorne teachers at a faculty meeting. The survey consisted of questions about the intern program, Core Knowledge, and the relationship between Trinity University and Hawthorne. The survey also allowed teachers to share their opinion on how these issues affect the faculty of Hawthorne, and more important, how each issue affects the students. The questions were rated on a scale of 1 to 5, with 5 being the best score. Next, teachers were interviewed at each grade level to gain a more personal idea of what the teachers felt about both programs. Teachers were asked questions about their experiences with the interns, the relationship between Trinity University and Hawthorne, and their opinions about the Core Knowledge program.

Overall, the results of the survey shed a positive light on the quality of both the Trinity program and Core Knowledge. Three questions shared a top score of 4.5. These questions were as follows: (a) "Rate the effect that Core Knowledge has had on your students' learning." (b) "Do you find the partnership with Trinity University useful/helpful?" and (c) "Do you feel that the partnership between Hawthorne and Trinity is a good model for other schools and universities?" This reflects teachers' approval of Core Knowledge and shows that the teachers have noticed a positive impact on their students' learning. This also shows that the teachers feel they have benefitted from their school's relationship with the university. The fact that teachers feel that the relationship is a good model reflects the success of the partnership.

The lowest average score on a survey item was a 3.2. That question was, "Is there adequate planning time for implementing the Core Knowledge program into teaching?" We concluded that, though many teachers do feel that Core Knowledge is very effective, they would also like to have more time for implementation. The teachers also were given space to provide personal comments. One teacher wrote, "Interns are a great asset to our school and provide excellent role models for our students." Another wrote, "Yes, this model has benefits for everyone (teachers, students, interns, etc.) involved!" See Table 1 for Hawthorne teachers' survey responses to the partnership.

TEACHER INTERVIEW RESULTS

Overall, the teachers interviewed at Hawthorne Elementary expressed approval of the intern program and Core Knowledge. Most teachers commented that they felt their interns were very professional and helpful. One positive comment repeated throughout the interviews was that the teachers could learn a variety of teaching techniques from their interns, or simply gain a fresh point of view. Also, interns helped to keep the mentor teachers up to date on current education issues, especially while discussing and reflecting on teacher practices. Many teachers, especially those in the lower levels, often commented that it was great to have another adult in the room to help out. One concern that several Hawthorne teachers discussed was that, due to program changes, they were now seeing fewer practicum students and some of the incoming interns now had fewer practicum hours than in the past. Most teachers felt that the program was better when more practicum hours were included.

Many teachers also expressed that Core Knowledge "levels the playing field" for the inner-city students at Hawthorne. Many students would not have exposure to certain cultural elements without this curriculum. Many teachers also explained that Core Knowledge builds from one grade level to the next instead of repeating the same subject material grade after grade. As one teacher explained, before Core Knowledge, a teacher would not know exactly what was taught in previous grade levels and therefore students received repetitive content. Without Core Knowledge, teachers explained, there could also be gaps in student learning. Fortunately, Hawthorne's curriculum lessens such gaps and repetitions. Though some teachers

TABLE 1
Survey of Teachers' Responses to the Partnership and Core Knowledge

Question	Average Score[a]
Rate the effect that Core Knowledge has had on your students' learning.	4.5
How easy/difficult was it to implement Core Knowledge into the required curriculum?	3.5
How much class time do you spend doing a Core Knowledge-related activity?	3.9
Have you noticed any improvements since Core Knowledge was implemented at Hawthorne?	4.1
Is there adequate planning time for implementing the Core Knowledge program into teaching?	3.2
How easy/difficult is it to acquire resources needed for Core Knowledge?	3.5
How beneficial are the Trinity University interns to the education of Hawthorne students?	4.2
Rate the professionalism and quality of work of the Trinity University interns.	4.3
Do you find the partnership with Trinity University useful/helpful?	4.5
Do you feel that the partnership between Hawthorne and Trinity University is a good model for other schools and universities?	4.5

[a]The highest possible score was 5.

did have a few minor complaints, such as needing certain materials or more time for implementation, each of them seemed to prefer Core Knowledge to other programs and conversed about it as a positive aspect of educating Hawthorne students.

SUMMARY AND IMPLICATIONS

Despite significant administrative and program changes, Hawthorne and Trinity University remain committed to the partnership, Core Knowledge, and the 5-year teacher education program. The Core Knowledge curriculum has withstood the test of time because of low teacher turnover and high student motivation. However, several major concerns must be addressed. The first is more hours of on-site practicum with increased involvement at a variety of levels and experiences. This is a concern frequently stated by students in the Early Childhood Education/Elementary program during recent interviews and discussions. The second issue is that the partnership must include all parties in major decisions and changes in the program, especially when there is a strong desire and commitment to do so. Advisory boards and communication strategies that inform and assist mentor teachers and interns in their roles and responsibilities in the partnership are imperative to continue the success of the Hawthorne Academy/Trinity University partnership, particularly if it is to last another 10 years, over which more leadership and program changes are inevitable.

REFERENCES

Core Knowledge Foundation. (2001). *Core knowledge sequence: Content guidelines for grades K–6.* Charlottesville, VA: Author.

Frazee, B. (1993). Core knowledge: How to get started. *Educational Leadership, 50,* 28–29.

Frazee, B. (1996). Hawthorne Elementary School: The university perspective. *Journal of Education for Students Placed At Risk, 1,* 25–31.

Holmes Group. (1986). *Tomorrow's teachers.* East Lansing, MI: Author.

Holmes Group. (1990). *Tomorrow's schools: Principles for the design of professional development schools.* East Lansing, MI: Author.

Johnston, S. (1994). Experience is the best teacher; or is it? An analysis of the role of experience in learning to teach. *Journal of Teacher Education, 45,* 199–208.

Koppich, J. (2000). Trinity University: Preparing teachers for tomorrow's schools. In L. Darling-Hammond (Ed.), *Studies of excellence in teacher education: Preparation in a five-year program* (pp. 1–95). New York: AACTE.

Putka, G. (1991, December 5). Making the grade. *The Wall Street Journal,* pp. 1, 22.

JOURNAL OF EDUCATION FOR STUDENTS PLACED AT RISK, *10*(2), 173–183

Hawthorne Academy:
The Evaluator's Perspective

Elda E. Martinez
Department of Education
Trinity University, and the
San Antonio Independent School District
San Antonio, TX

BACKGROUND

Hawthorne Academy, in San Antonio, Texas, serves approximately 550 students from the 3-year-old pre-K through the eighth grade. Previously a traditional elementary school, Hawthorne was granted an internal charter beginning in the 2001–2002 school year. Fundamental components of the charter include the following: providing open enrollment to students from within Bexar County, a full-day preschool for 3- and 4-year-olds, the addition of the middle school grades, and the continuation of the Core Knowledge curriculum. The middle school grades enroll approximately 50 students per grade, beginning with the sixth grade in the 2002–2003 academic year, culminating with the addition of the eighth-grade cohort in the 2004–2005 school year.

As one of 63 elementary schools and 17 middle schools in the San Antonio Independent School District (SAISD), Hawthorne is an inner-city campus serving a predominantly working-class population. In accordance with the charter agreement, open enrollment has allowed students from outside of the district to attend the school. In the 2003–2004 school year, 514 students are enrolled from pre-K through seventh grade; 43 come from outside the district.

Campus demographics are similar to those of the district's 57,108 students (as of October 2003). The ethnic composition of the district's student body was predominantly Hispanic at 86.5%, followed by Black (not Hispanic) at 9.3%, White (not Hispanic) at 3.8%, Asian at 0.2%, and American Indian at 0.1%. The 2003 demographic profile for Hawthorne's student body of 500 showed 84.4% Hispanic,

Requests for reprints should be sent to Elda E. Martinez, 8219 Budge Drive, San Antonio, TX 78240. E-mail: eldamartinez@satx.rr.com

8.4% White, 5.8% African American, 1.4% Pacific Islander, and 0% Native American. The 2003 data also indicates a larger number of Limited English Proficient students, 24.6% at the campus (n = 123) compared to the district's 18.9%. The Special Education program at the campus served 13.6% of the student body (n = 68) compared to the district's 12.8%. It is also important to note that, of the 500 students enrolled in the 2002–2003 school year, 90.6% (n = 453) were identified as economically disadvantaged. This number, though large, mirrored the district's 90.2% of economically disadvantaged students. Initiatives at Hawthorne allowed for a 14.6 to 1 student–teacher ratio, slightly lower than the 16 to 1 district ratio.

Historically, Texas schools have had to administer standardized tests to students beginning in the third and running through the eighth grades and at the high school exit level. During the period of 1994–2002, the Texas Assessment of Academic Skills (TAAS) was administered. The Texas Education Agency revised the test in 2003 with the administration of the Texas Assessment of Knowledge and Skills test (TAKS). As its predecessor, the TAKS test is a criterion-referenced evaluation assessing students' mastery of the state standards in reading and math. In addition, the writing test is administered to fourth and seventh graders; fifth graders must also take the science test; and eighth graders take the Social Studies portion. At the high school level, students must pass the exit level tests in order to graduate. Implementation of the TAKS test proved to be a challenge as the test design focused more on implicit questioning than the previous TAAS test. Though data from both tests have been included to illustrate the difference between campus and district performance, it is important to note that the test was designed with an increasing passing standard during each administration of TAKS testing.

METHOD

To gain an understanding of Hawthorne's academic performance in relation to the Core Knowledge curriculum, test data have been assessed from 1993 through 2003. This 10-year period begins with the 1st year of Core Knowledge implementation and ends with the 2003 test data. At the time of the writing of this article, official test scores had not been published for the 2004 testing. Preliminary 2004 test data have been used in the longitudinal view of the seventh-grade cohort (see Figures 8 and 9). TAAS results are used for the 1993–2002 school years, whereas TAKS results are used for the 2003–2004 school years. Hawthorne's campus information is compared to the district performance for students in the third- through seventh-grade classes and is reported in terms of the percentage of students passing minimum standards at the indicated grade level.

As in the original article from the evaluator's perspective (Schubnell, 1996), two methods of analysis will be used. First, longitudinal views of each grade level's performance are compared to the district's performance for students at the same grade level. Though this does not indicate changing passing standards for each test administration, this does allow an overview of grade-level performance over a 10-year time span in relation to the aggregate performance of all other elementary schools in the district. This information is not a matched student analysis in that each year of testing reflects the performance of a different cohort of students. Test data reported is for reading and math for Grades 3 though 7, as well as the Grade 4 writing test. Though the seventh grade also takes the writing test, these data were not included, as the official scores for the 2004 test administration have not yet been received.

The second method of analysis looks at the achievement of the oldest cohort of students, the seventh graders of the 2004 school year. This longitudinal study provides the matched student analysis that indicates student growth from third through seventh grades as measured by the percentage of students meeting minimum standards for each year. For this purpose, data from the reading and mathematics test were used. The writing test was not included, as it is not administered annually.

RESULTS

Three methods of presentation are used to present the findings of this data analysis. First, annual snapshots of the students meeting passing standards for each grade, third through fifth, illustrate a comparison of campus performance to district performance in both reading and mathematics (see Figures 1–7). Each graph shows how the respective grade level performed over a 10-year time span (1993–2003). Second, the percentage of students meeting passing standards in a student cohort document the matched student analysis over a period of 5 years, from their third- through seventh-grade academic years (see Figures 8–9). These graphs present both reading and mathematics performance, comparing campus achievement to district achievement. Third, a multiyear performance history compares the number of all students tested passing all tests taken at the campus, district, and state levels (see Figure 10). This graph documents the growth at each level on the TAAS test for the period of 1994–2002. Due to the recent introduction of the TAKS test, there is not sufficient data available to distinguish the performance growth on the 2003 and 2004 test administrations.

School and District Snapshots of Annual
TAAS/TAKS Results (1994–2004)

Figures 1 and 2 show Hawthorne's third-grade performance on standardized testing from 1994–2003 in comparison to district third graders. Figure 1 shows a steady increase in the district's third-grade performance. Hawthorne third-grade classes have been inconsistent, showing a variation in scores alternating from above district results to below district results. It is important to note that it was expected that the first administration of the TAKS test in 2003 would result in a decline in test scores. Rather, Hawthorne students, compared to a mere 5.1% increase in the district average, realized a 20.6% increase. Preliminary results of the 2004 TAKS administration

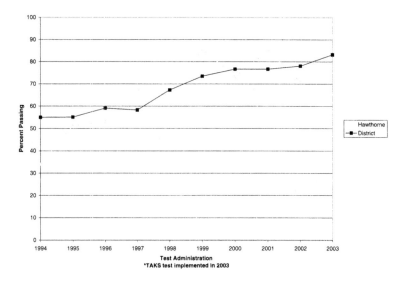

FIGURE 1   Third-grade reading standardized testing, 1994–2003.

show 91% mastery at the campus third-grade level. Figure 2 shows a steady increase in the district's third-grade mathematics performance. Though Hawthorne has seen a 44.2% increase in scores over the 10-year period, scores have continued to fall below the district mean since the significant 18.7% decline in 2000.

Figures 3, 4, and 5 show Hawthorne's fourth-grade performance on standardized testing from 1994 through 2003 in comparison to district fourth graders. Figure 3 de-

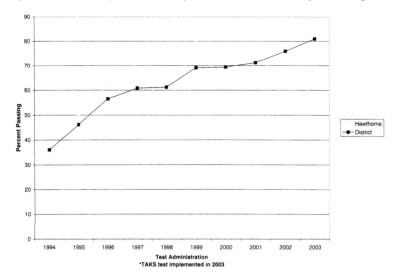

FIGURE 2   Third-grade mathematics standardized testing, 1994–2003.

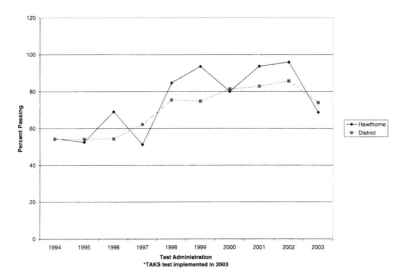

FIGURE 3   Fourth-grade reading standardized testing, 1994–2003.

scribes the performance of Hawthorne fourth graders in reading compared to the district mean. Overall, the district's results show a steady increase with an exception in 2003. Again, this was the 1st year of the TAKS test administration; due to the design of the test, a decline was expected. Hawthorne also showed a decline, falling below the district average despite scoring higher than the district in the 2 years prior to the first administration of the TAKS test. The significant drops were in 1997 (18%),

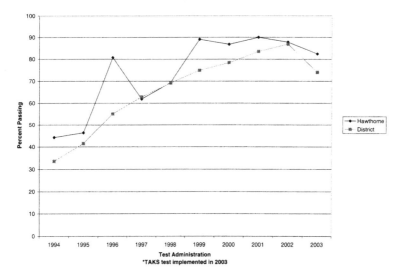

FIGURE 4   Fourth-grade mathematics standardized testing, 1994–2003.

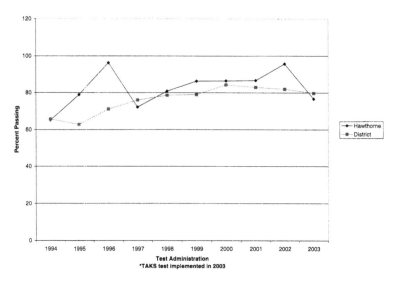

FIGURE 5   Fourth-grade writing standardized testing, 1994–2003.

2000 (13.5%), and 2003 (27.1%). Figure 4 describes fourth-grade performance on the mathematics test. Hawthorne students consistently scored above the district mean. Although scoring below the district by 1% in 1997, there is not a significant difference. A notable increase is apparent in 1996 (34.5%) from the 1995 performance score. This cohort of students also realized a 16.7% increase in the third grade on the mathematics test. Figure 5 presents a similar finding on the writing test as on the fourth-grade reading and mathematics tests. Scores dropped in 1997 on all subject tests. A review of the student cohort's performance at the third-grade level in 1996 shows that there is less than a 1% range on the 1996 and 1997 testing in reading and mathematics. Considering the increase in difficulty of the test content, this particular cohort of students remained stable in their testing performance.

Figures 6 and 7 show Hawthorne's fifth-grade performance on standardized testing from 1994 through 2003 in comparison to district fifth graders. Figure 6 shows scores that more consistently reflect similar patterns between Hawthorne and the district. With less fluctuation, both sets of scores have shown general increases. As with the fourth-grade tests, fifth graders showed a decline in the 1997 administration. Unlike the fourth-grade results, this decline was minimal (4.7% difference from 1996) and did not fall below the district mean. The first TAKS test administration in 2003 resulted in a decline at both the campus and district levels; yet the Hawthorne difference at 12.5% was less severe than the 18.9% district difference when compared to the last TAAS test administration in 2002. Figure 7 illustrates fifth-grade performance on mathematics testing. In accordance with the fifth-grade reading test scores, there is less variation between campus and district scores than at the other grade levels. The observation of a decline in 1997 is again present.

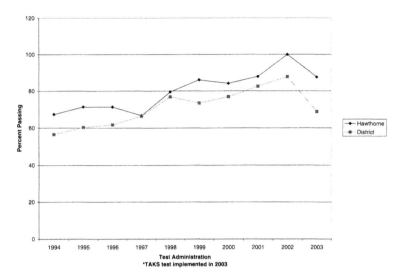

FIGURE 6   Fifth-grade reading standardized testing, 1994–2003.

TAAS/TAKS Performance Results for Matched
Samples of Students (2000–2004)

The matched student analysis follows a cohort of students from third grade to seventh grade. This is the first group of students to progress through the Hawthorne middle school. Historically, the test results for the middle school grades show a significant decline across the SAISD. One of the fundamental reasons for adding

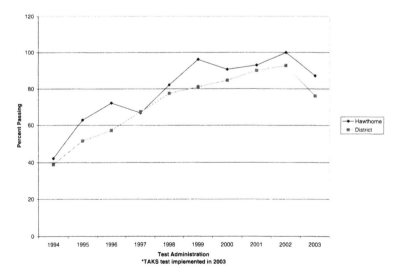

FIGURE 7   Fifth-grade mathematics standardized testing, 1994–2003.

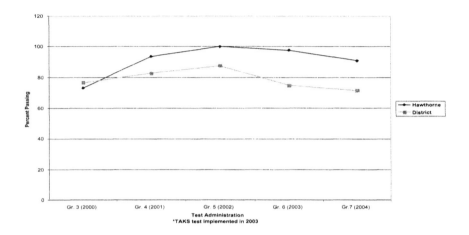

FIGURE 8   Longitudianal view of student growth, reading standardized testing.

the middle school as part of the charter agreement was to remedy the drop in test results at the middle school level. Preliminary results are used for the 2004 data. Figures 8 and 9 show results for the reading and mathematics test, respectively.

This cohort of students participated in the Core Knowledge curriculum throughout their elementary and current middle school education. Though the district's cohort of students continued to demonstrate growth on the TAAS test from 2000 through 2002, the Hawthorne cohort did so with greater gains. The expected

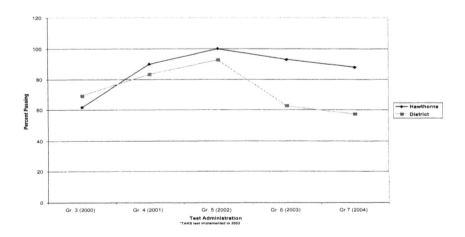

FIGURE 9   Longitudianal study of student growth, mathematics standardized testing.

decline in the percentage of passing scores with the administration of the TAKS test was realized but with a significant difference; whereas the district saw a 12.7% decrease (from 87.7% in 2002 to 75% in 2003), Hawthorne saw only a 2.3% decrease (from 100% in 2002 to 97.7% in 2003). As the test difficulty increases, as does the passing standard with each TAKS administration, Hawthorne students continue to surpass the performance of their district peers.

The cohort's performance on the mathematics test shows more dramatic results than the reading test. Again, a decrease was realized between administrations of the TAAS and the TAKS test for both groups. The district dropped 30.2% from 2002 through 2003 (92.8% to 62.6%), but the Hawthorne group dropped only 7% (100% to 93%). Though various interventions and programs were implemented in the time these students have been in school, the one distinct difference is that the Hawthorne students had the Core Knowledge curriculum while no other district school did.

Multiyear Performance History on TAAS Testing (1994–2002)

Figure 10 provides a visual for a multiyear perspective of total student achievement on standardized testing at the Hawthorne campus in comparison to district and state results. This data applies to the 9 years that TAAS was administered. These scores are a composite of all grade levels and all tests taken. It is interesting to note a continued increase, except for the 2000 test administration. Over the 9-year time span, Hawthorne experienced a 54% increase in campus performance. This result was noteworthy when compared to the district change of +43.3% and the state change of +29.7%. Though Hawthorne continues to fall behind the state average, the difference continues to decrease. In 1994, Hawthorne fell 26.6% behind the state average of all students passing all areas of the TAAS test. By 2002, only a 2.3% difference

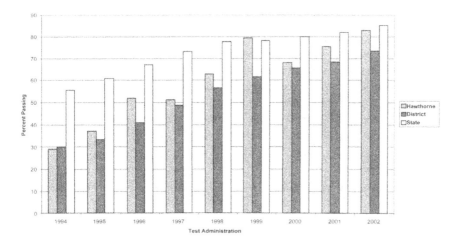

FIGURE 10   Multi-year performance history.

was present. Consider the district—state comparisons of 25.6% in 2002 and 12% in 2004 and, once again, it is apparent that Hawthorne's initiatives and programming are promoting student performance and increasing academic achievement.

DISCUSSION

This study aimed to determine the effect of Core Knowledge on student achievement. The data analysis of student performance on the TAAS and TAKS tests spanned 10 years. Core Knowledge was first implemented at Hawthorne during the 1992–1993 academic year. At that time, a previous version of standardized testing was in place. The Texas Educational Assessment of Minimum Skills (TEAMS) test evaluated reading, writing, and mathematics skills, just as its successors have. However, this assessment program focused on minimum skills as opposed to evaluating academic skills. Therefore, it was not appropriate to include TEAMS data in this study.

The data presented for the 1993–1994 academic year, therefore, reflected the progress made after the 2nd year of Core Knowledge implementation. Although each grade level presented both increases and decreases in student performance on the standardized testing,[1] the fluctuation minimized at the upper grade levels. This may be due to increased student comfort with the testing instrument, growth of students' knowledge base, and the spiraling effects of the Core Knowledge curriculum. Though Core Knowledge cannot be identified as the sole variable responsible for the campus performance growth, it has been the consistent program among various programs implemented and ended throughout the 10 years. If the district's students are seen as a control group benefitting from district-mandated programs, then Hawthorne's students can be seen as a treatment group—partaking in the same district-mandated programs but with the addition of the Core Knowledge curriculum.

Changes in test design and in the increasing passing standards for each year may impact results as much as variables in student cohorts. Therefore, though the grade-level snapshots (see Figures 1–7) may provide information on grade-specific instructional practices, the longitudinal data following a specific cohort of students may be a more accurate indicator of the increase in student achievement. Although there is not yet sufficient data to include middle school achievement scores as grade-level snapshots, indicators show that student cohorts are continuing to improve. Consider also the multiyear history on the TAAS test. Clearly, the striking

---

[1]Such fluctuation was to be expected given the small sample of students at any given grade in the school.

54% increase from a 29% passing rate (all students tested passing all tests taken) in 1994 to an 83% passing rate in 2002 is indicative of effective interventions.

An additional observation of test data reflects an occurrence during the 1998–2000 era. A dramatically significant increase is present when comparing the 1998 results to 1999. This increase is observed in every grade level on each test administered. This is of particular interest when the 2000 test data are reviewed, as a significant decrease is present at all grade levels on each test, with the exception of the fourth-grade writing test, which remained constant. The multiyear performance history (see Figure 10) replicates this finding. Hawthorne demonstrated a consistent and steady increase, with the exception of a significant decline in school performance in 2000; this decline was not realized at either the district or state levels. The growth indicator the previous year in 1999 was the greatest in the 10-year span at a 16.8% increase, far surpassing the growth rates at the district or state levels. Whereas no specific variable can be identified by analysis of the test data, there may be some correlation in the administrative and curricular changes at the school during this time. The "Age of Deletion" (see Mentzer & Shaughessy, in this issue) marked a period of inconsistency in curricular practices, including the level of Core Knowledge implementation.

The original evaluation by Gail Schubnell in 1996 suggested a curriculum-sequencing effect, citing "that achievement builds upon itself at successive grade levels" (p. 39). It is evident that Hawthorne is making substantial gains compared to district students at each consecutive grade level. Analysis of student cohorts over time appears to support the notion that curriculum sequencing and increased content knowledge development will continue to lead to increased student achievement. Despite the large number of economically disadvantaged students coming to Hawthorne, it is clear that the added variable of Core Knowledge is enriching the students' educational experience and resulting in increased academic achievement.

REFERENCE

Schubnell, G. (1996). Hawthorne Elementary School: The evaluator's perspective. *Journal of Education for Students Placed At Risk, 1,* 33–40.

JOURNAL OF EDUCATION FOR STUDENTS PLACED AT RISK, *10*(2), 185–197

Essentials of Literacy:
From A Pilot Site at Davis Street School
To District-Wide Intervention

Fay E. Brown
Child Study Center
Yale University

Edward T. Murray
School of Education
Sacred Heart University

Since the mid 1990s, reading instruction has changed and so has the School Development Program's (SDP) Essentials of Literacy (EOL) process. Beginning as a teaching suggestion at one New Haven, Connecticut school, Lincoln Bassett, EOL became a pilot project at Davis Street School in New Haven for the 1996–1997 school year and continues to be an implemented model in that school. Due to the results the program yielded at Davis, it was expanded to several other schools in the district and, for the last 4 years, has been the district's accepted intervention model.

In the 1994–1995 school year, Davis Street Magnet school began participating in the New Haven School District's effort to comprehensively renew and strengthen the implementation of the School Development Program (SDP). Over the next couple of years, while trying to effectively put in place all the different components of the model, Davis recognized its need for an intervention reading program and decided to allow the SDP to pilot its newly developed EOL intervention reading program at the school.

During that pilot year, the 1996–1997 school year, both authors spent a significant amount of time in the school providing consultation and coaching to the staff. We witnessed and documented many instances of successes of the staff, students, and parents, including, for example, changes in students' behavior and in their atti-

Requests for reprints should be sent to Fay E. Brown, Yale School Development Program, 230 South Frontage Road, New Haven, CT 06520. E-mail: fay.brown@yale.edu

tudes toward reading and the willingness of some students to persevere through a challenging task on which they might have given up prior to participating in EOL. We also witnessed and documented some challenges on the part of the leadership and staff in effectively implementing the program, including the issue of funding to provide all the materials to implement the program and the challenge of maintaining a consistent staff, as the school was relying on volunteers to facilitate certain aspects of the program (Brown, Maholmes, Murray, & Nathan, 1998).

Focusing more on their successes and finding creative means to handle their challenges, the school experienced a positive year with the pilot project. That year, 24 third-grade students participated in the program, all of whom were reading at either a kindergarten or first-grade level. The program started in September, and by March, over 50% of those students were reading at or near grade level (Brown et al., 1998). The results of that first year fueled the energy and commitment of the leadership and staff to continue to implement the program. Their success ignited a strong interest across the district that has led to the current status of EOL as the district's intervention reading program.

To assist the reader in gaining a better understanding of EOL and of Davis Street school, this article will focus on the following: an overview of literature that underscores the importance of reading ability; a brief description of EOL, including some objectives of the program; a revisit to Davis with particular attention to some of the changes the school has experienced over the years; and a perspective that highlights outcomes of EOL beyond Davis—to the broader New Haven school district and to several other schools outside of New Haven.

Reading ability is increasingly a prerequisite for success in today's society. The 2002 RAND Report on Reading Comprehension states, "the U.S. economy today demands a universally higher level of literacy achievement than at any other time in history, and it is reasonable to believe that the demand for a literate populace will increase in the future" (p. 4). Some researchers argue that reading is not a natural process (Shaywitz, 2003); rather, it is a process that must be learned. However, for students to learn to read, and ultimately to read to learn, they must be taught to do so. Hill (1998) and Beers (2003) have highlighted the need for a better understanding of the instructional strategies that help struggling students become successful readers.

IMPORTANCE OF READING ABILITY

Children who do not transition well from "learning to read" to "reading to learn" (i.e., using reading skills to acquire understanding of new content across subject areas) are unable to participate fully in or learn effectively from instruction. Long-term struggling readers are more likely to perform poorly in school, drop out of school, or not attain higher education; face greater employment challenges; and are heavily over-represented among delinquents and incarcerated youth and adults (Cornwall & Bawden, 1992; Slavin, 1998; Werner, 1993). The problem is compounded when students who are poor readers or who dislike reading become parents; due to their own alienation from reading, they pass this aversion on to their children (Beers, 1998).

Longitudinal studies show that 74% of children diagnosed as reading disabled in third grade remain disabled in ninth grade (Fletcher et al., 1994; Shaywitz, Escobar, Shaywitz, Fletcher, & Makuch, 1992; Stanovich & Siegel, 1994). Making a similar argument, Grosso De León (2002) pointed out that "failing to master the skills necessary to read to learn, students who slip into the fourth-grade slump can and, more often than not, do find themselves headed for the eighth-grade cliff, when academic content becomes increasingly diverse and complex" (p. 5). In her most recent work, Shaywitz (2003) stated that

> Reading disabilities diagnosed after third grade are much more difficult to remediate. Early identification is important because the brain is much more plastic in younger children and potentially more malleable for the rerouting of neural circuits. Moreover, once a child falls behind, he must make up thousands of unread words to catch up to his peers who are continuing to move ahead. Equally important, once a pattern of reading sets in, many children become defeated, lose interest in reading, and develop what often evolves into a lifelong loss of their own sense of self-worth. (p. 31)

Appropriate and early direct instruction can prevent reading difficulties in a population of children who are at risk for reading failure (Adams, 1991; Beck & Juel, 1995). Although not a magic cure, over the past 10 years, the School Development Program of the Yale Child Study Center has been assisting schools in implementing an enrichment reading program, the EOL program, which has been yielding outstanding results for a significant number of students.

THE ESSENTIALS OF LITERACY PROCESS

EOL is an elementary-level reading intervention program that brings together the child-centered strategies of the Comer process with research-based instructional strategies to improve the literacy skills of struggling elementary level students. This program is built on the premise that eight "essentials" or fundamentals of literacy constitute a successful reading program. They are as follows: Story Sense, Vocabulary Development, Book Immersion (Guided Reading), Story Writing and Publishing, Phonics Instruction, Meaningful Teacher–Student Ratio, Consistent Monitoring of Students' Progress, and Home/School Reinforcement. EOL consists of small group instruction, various stations among which students rotate, a wide range of engaging materials, and frequent assessment to monitor students' progress.

The EOL process comprises many of the elements that were recommended in the report of the National Reading Panel in 2000 (phonemic awareness, phonics, fluency, vocabulary instruction, guided oral reading, text comprehension, and technology). As a member of that panel, Shaywitz (2003) echoed the recommendations of the Panel by stating that "programs that teach phonics systematically and explicitly are most effective" (p. 210). Explicit phonics instruction is one of the key components of the EOL process.

An added value of the EOL process is that it takes into consideration the individual variation of all the students who are selected for the program and uses an eclectic approach to help develop their literacy skills. Furthermore, the process promotes development along the six critical pathways that form the foundation of the model of the School Development Program—physical, cognitive, language, social, ethical, and psychological. As children learn to read, their self-esteem is strengthened and they learn and demonstrate positive behaviors that foster achievement. This kind of interaction effect was also noted by Beers (2003) in her writing about the different kinds of confidences that readers need. She pointed out that "what's critical to note is that as one area [of confidence] improves, others do too. When we are working with students, the areas commingle, creating a ricochet effect—attending to one issue creates a momentum that ricochets to another confidence" (p. 17).

EOL was designed to be integrated into the school's language arts program, and it fosters students' literacy development in an environment that is nonthreatening and highly rewarding. A primary goal of the program is to expose students to as many stories and books as possible. On any given day, a student in an EOL classroom can be exposed to 5 books a day, 25 a week, 100 a month, 1,000 in a year. One goal here is to help bridge the gap for many of the children who are starting at a disadvantage in terms of their preparation for acquisition of words. As noted by Hart and Risley (2003), by age 3, there is about a 20 million-word gap between a child from a professional or more affluent family and a child from a working-class family, and a 30 million-word gap for a child from a welfare family. Perhaps more alarming is that their study revealed that measures of accomplishments for these 3-year-olds actually predicted measures of language skill at ages 9 to 10. Thus, for these students, there is a need for intervention programs that can help to ameliorate such disparate circumstances.

Another goal in exposing students in an EOL classroom to so many books and stories is to help students develop a schema so that comprehension can be achieved. A story to begin the day (Story Station), a story during guided reading (Guided Reading Station), a story to listen to (Listening Station), a story to write (Writing and Publishing Station), a book to take home to read with or to a parent or guardian—these are all essential components of literacy in the EOL program. Besides building background, students in an EOL classroom are provided with daily coaching sessions. During guided reading, the focus is on one-to-one instruction where students are matched to leveled books that they read aloud to their reading coach. The coach focuses on fluency and comprehension and prompting students to corrective responses.

The work on whole language (Goodman, 1986) has solidified the reading–writing connection. In EOL, the writing process complements phonics instruction, word recognition, and word-building skills. Although early reading is based on recognizing patterns and word families, the skill of writing, utilizing invented spellings, and the focus on letter-by-letter construction are all strategies that help students to focus their attention on the details and conventions of our language. These processes help students to understand that writing is "talk written down." The process adds value and worth to the language and experiences that students bring to the table. Additionally, in an EOL classroom, the publishing of students' early efforts, which they read aloud and share with others, is unsurpassed in validating their progress in becoming successful readers.

SPECIFIC PROJECT OBJECTIVES

In addition to the precepts of the EOL process previously described, the process also aims to accomplish the following specific objectives:

• *Collaborative engagement of teachers:* Building on the work of the Comer process, particularly the guiding principles of collaboration, consensus, and no-fault problem solving, teachers ensure that the program is not being implemented in isolation from the school's overall efforts to promote literacy. Sharing research-based strategies, teachers work together to match students with the most effective instructional techniques, thereby creating a positive learning environment.

• *Child-centered approach in interacting with students:* Adults who work in an EOL classroom are taught how to utilize the six developmental pathways—cognitive, physical, language, social, psychological, and ethical—as a framework to guide their interactions, instruction, and assessment of the students. The understanding fostered is that when students reach third and fourth grade and are unable to read or are struggling immensely, intervention has to go beyond simply teaching reading strategies; it must encompass ways of nurturing and promoting learning and development, and, at times, even repairing damaged self-esteem. This pathways framework enables parents, teachers, and community volunteers to promote literacy within the broader context of knowledge of how children develop and learn.

• *Improved student achievement:* Over the years, EOL has resulted in notable improvements in students' reading skills, as demonstrated by different measurements like the Developmental Reading Assessment (DRA), which is utilized in the New Haven school district. For the school years 1999–2000 and 2001–2002, students in New Haven's EOL program gained an average of 1.5 to 2 years' growth in reading during a 7-month period. Similar results were obtained from schools in Old Westbury, New York and Union City, New Jersey.

• *Improved behavior and attitudes:* A major assumption of this process is that, as students start to experience success in their reading, there will be a demonstrable decrease in problem behavior for those identified as exhibiting such behaviors. This assumption has been upheld by EOL personnel in several schools. For example, one teacher at Park Avenue school in Westbury commented that "The students not only progressed in their reading, but the increase in self-esteem was also noted. Students, feeling competent, changed their behavior! There was a great reduction in the negative behavior episodes of the students receiving the EOL instruction." Evidence of such improved behaviors were observed in an earlier study from data collected through the use of the Teacher–Child Rating Scale from the pilot school in New Haven (Brown et al., 1998).

• *Increased parent involvement:* A key element of the EOL Reading Room is daily involvement of parents and community volunteers who sometimes facilitate and monitor selected learning stations, such as the Listening or Story station. This involvement generates continuity between home and school. Parents learn how to help their children at home and they develop their own literacy skills. Additionally, because students are expected to take a book home every night to read with or to a parent or caregiver, more books are made available to homes that may otherwise not have access to such materials.

• *Increased adult–student ratio:* In many urban schools, class sizes are so large it is difficult for students to get the attention they need to strengthen specific skills. Such over-crowdedness is particularly detrimental for students who are at risk of failure. The EOL process enables small groups of students to work daily with an adult on a variety of literacy skills. An effectively staffed EOL room has 24 to 30 students working in groups of four or five at six stations, each facilitated by an adult. This design also allows for flexible grouping, so that a child can move in or out of a group depending on his or her progress and skill level.

• *Integrated research-based teaching strategies with instructional software:* EOL allows schools the flexibility of incorporating technology into their reading room. At the station, students have the opportunity to utilize instructional software based on the latest research and best teaching practices. These practices foster reading, writing, and overall language arts skills development.

Since the days of being piloted at Davis Street school, EOL has evolved into an established intervention program for struggling readers in several elementary schools. The lessons learned along the way have served as a foundation for the articulation of the aforementioned objectives and have provided insightful changes that continue to make a difference at Davis and beyond.

Davis Street Magnet School: Then and Now

Davis Street Inter-District Magnet School serves a population of approximately 340 kindergarten through fifth-grade students. Since 1998, when we first published our case study of Davis Street (Brown et al., 1998), there has been a slight decline in student population due in part to changes at the district level. Five new schools have been constructed in the district and several Grade 6–8 schools have been changed to K–8 schools. This decline in student body numbers at Davis has led to a reduction of class size for most classes. Whereas a few years ago there was an average of 26 students per class, there is now an average of 18 students in most classes. The school's inter-district magnet status has also resulted in some changes in the school. In the past, the students at Davis came mainly from the school community. Now, students are bused in from several neighboring districts such as Ansonia, East Haven, Guilford, Hamden, Milford, and West Haven. The racial composition of the students has changed slightly, with about 70% of the student body being African American.

The school continues to experience its successes and challenges, just like most other schools in the New Haven school district. Several changes have been seen in the area of staffing over the years. During the 1997–1998 school year, Davis lost about five teachers who were promoted within the district as math or literacy mentors, with one becoming the supervisor of reading for the district. The principal, Mrs. Lola Nathan, a veteran at Davis for 13 years and a strong and positive presence in the school, explains that over the next 3 years she had "a transient teaching staff, more like a revolving door of teachers. A few teachers would stay for one year and then leave to another district" (personal communication, September 28, 2004). One of the main causes for this turnover was a major contract change that many teachers, particularly new teachers, felt did not offer them and their families the benefits they desired. Mrs. Nathan adds that the school—operating by the principles of the Comer process of collaboration, consensus, and no-fault problem solving—made it through those challenging years. One standard that remained unchanged even during those challenging years was that of making decisions that were in the best interest of the students. One decision was to continue to implement EOL. The results analyzed for the school year 1999–2000 showed that Davis continued to experience success with the program (see Figure 1).

Data were collected from the Developmental Reading Assessment (DRA) at different periods throughout the year. The DRA is an assessment tool used by teachers on an annual, semiannual, or quarterly basis to observe, record, and evaluate changes in students' reading. It is also used by teachers to plan ways of individually and meaningfully working with students to help them improve their reading. Assessment texts represent a range of difficulty, from Level A to Level 44. Levels A through 2 represent kindergarten; 3 through 8 represent preprimer; 10 through 12 represent primer; 14 through 16 represent first grade; 18 through 28 represent second grade; 30 through 38 represent third grade; 40 represents fourth grade; and 44 represents fifth grade (Beaver, 1997; Brown, 2004).

As can be observed from Figure 1, at the beginning of the year, students in the EOL program at Davis Street School had a 7.9 mean DRA score, which indicates a preprimer reading level. In January, students had a mean score of 12.2, which indicates a primer level, and by May of that year, they improved in their reading to an 18.8 mean score, which is a second-grade level. For the May score, individual student scores ranged from 12 to 30. For the 2003–2004 school year, 22 students participated in the EOL program that was implemented at the second-grade level. Col-

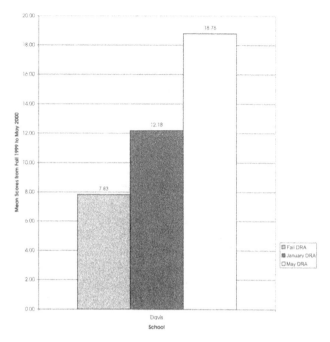

FIGURE 1   Improvement in reading scores for students in Essentials of Literacy Reading Rooms using the Developmental Reading Assessment (DRA).

lected data have not yet been analyzed, as in the past, but preliminary findings are as follows: At the beginning of the year, 40% (9) of the students were reading below first grade (DRA Levels 2–12); 40% were reading at first grade (Levels 14–16); and 18% (4) were reading at second grade (Level 18). By May, nearly every student demonstrated improvement in their reading, with 9% (2) reading below first grade (Level 6), about 4.5% (1) reading at first grade, 36% (8) reading at second grade, and 50% (11) reading at third grade. It should be noted that one limitation of the DRA is that it is teacher-scored and, like most other assessments scored by individuals, scores can be inflated or deflated. As researchers, in the absence of conducting controlled studies, we rely on the honesty and integrity of the people from whom we collect our data.

Implementing EOL at the second as opposed to the third grade is just one of the recent changes that Davis has made. According to Mrs. Nathan, "Davis is at a better place now" than it was at the time of the publication of the EOL pilot study. She explains some of those changes as follows:

Over the last 3 years, Davis can be defined as being stable in terms of quality staff and quality teaching. There has been more of a focus on small group instruction and the design of Individualized Education Plans (IEPs) for all students. IEPs are not just for the special education population, but must be designed for all students. At Davis, we have IEPs starting at Kindergarten through Grade 5 because we have to get our kindergartners ready for first grade. Then we have to identify the areas of need or weakness for each student and help each child to gain the skills needed for success.

We are more knowledgeable about using data to inform our decision making. The staff has received training on analyzing and interpreting data, and on how to develop effective strategies to assist students in mastering specific skills. Based on data, we have started to implement EOL in second grade because we have found that many students needed that intervention earlier than third grade. This change has proven extremely successful in that, for the first time since the district started its mandatory summer program for students needing the added intervention, none of Davis' students needed to attend. This situation is in contrast to 5 years ago, when almost 50% of the third graders attended summer school. The bottom line is that we have become more sophisticated in the delivery of services to our children. We are not perfect. We still have a way to go; as a matter of fact, I need about 2 more years to put in place some of the other changes I would like to see here at Davis. (personal communication, September 28, 2004)

From being successfully implemented in one reading room at Davis Street, EOL was expanded to 10 schools in the 1998–1999 school year, and to 23 schools in the 1999–2000 school year. The program is currently being implemented in 20 schools in the district, with some schools implementing it at two grade levels—second and third. The implementation of the program has helped the district to achieve some important changes in reading across its elementary schools. Some of these changes are described in the following section by Eleanor Osborne, the Associate Superintendent of schools for the district (personal communication, September 17, 2004).

Perspective From the Associate Superintendent of Schools

When I first came to the New Haven school district in 1997 and examined the status of reading across the district, what I found was a high level of fragmentation in programs and services and a high percentage of students reading below grade level. At that time, 85% of third graders were reading significantly below grade level with 27% of them not knowing letter–sound correspondence. I knew that my first priority was to effect some changes to improve the reading skills of a significant percentage of our students across the district.

In exploring my choices, someone advised me to visit Davis Street school to observe what they were doing with a new reading program for their struggling readers. I was impressed with what I saw at Davis and more impressed when I examined the data and noted the students' performance on the Connecticut Mastery Test (CMT). This new reading program, EOL, was providing students the individualized instruction they needed in the core elements of literacy (story sense, phonics, vocabulary, guided reading/comprehension, and writing) in an environment that also promoted their social and psychological development. Additionally, the program provided the teachers and the aides, including parent volunteers, training to effectively execute the various components of the program, yet allowing the flexibility for teacher creativity and for the integration of certain district requirements into the model.

Though some individuals in the district were advocating for me to bring in specific basal readers to effect change in reading, I disagreed because I was not interested in promoting a book company, but needed teachers to learn how to effectively teach students how to read. The EOL program fulfilled that objective. So, as part of the district's comprehensive plan, I phased in EOL in 23 elementary schools within the next couple of school years. Ten schools implemented the program in school year 1998–1999 and 23 schools implemented it in school year 1999–2000. Each school that implemented the program achieved significant results in the space of 7 months, with demonstrable results within 3 months. Data collected from the 1999–2000 administration of the Developmental Reading Assessment revealed that, across the district, students who participated in EOL gained a year-and-a-half to 2 years' improvement in their reading within 7 months (see Figure 2).

The success of EOL throughout the school year prompted the decision to model the district's mandatory summer school program after the EOL program. For Summer School 1999–2000, for the 5-week program, we implemented a modified version of EOL. The success of that program was phenomenal. With over 600 stu-

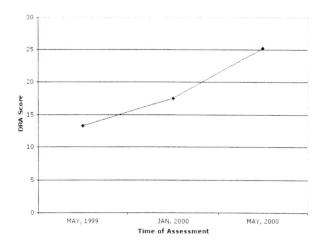

FIGURE 2   Developmental Reading Assessment (DRA) scores for New Haven students participating in Essentials of Literacy ($N = 548$).

dents participating in the program, there was an average gain of 7 months' reading at the end of those 5 weeks. Over the years, we have continued that same model for summer school, each year obtaining similar results.

For the first time in the district, in the 2002–2003 school year, 79% of third graders were promoted to fourth-grade reading on or above grade level. This school year, that figure was increased to 82%. An important index of student performance is the state's standardized test, which in this state is the Connecticut Mastery Test (CMT). Based on students' performance on that test, results are distributed within three categories: intervention, proficient, and excellent. For many years, the greatest concentration of New Haven's elementary students was in the intervention category. Within the past 2 years, with the different efforts across the district, including the continued implementation of EOL, the district has experienced an 11% decrease in that intervention category. We are proud of the outcomes we have experienced in the district in the area of reading for our students, and I credit our dedicated staff for their continued hard work and for their willingness and flexibility in implementing models like EOL. I also credit them for their wisdom in using data to drive their instructional practices and decision making (personal communication, September 17, 2004).

EOL Beyond New Haven

The success of EOL in New Haven has led to its implementation in several other school districts, though not on the same scale as in New Haven. For example, the program is being implemented in schools in Union City, Paterson, and Pemberton, New Jersey, and in three schools in Old Westbury, New York. Some of these schools have had results similar to those in New Haven, whereas others have had some struggles along the way. For example, Park Avenue school in Old Westbury started out 3 years ago by implementing EOL in one classroom. The success in that school of the program over time has caused the school to now implement the program in three classrooms. That success has also sparked the interest of two other elementary schools in the district that are currently implementing the program.

In places where the staff has experienced struggles, observations of their implementation and interviews with them generally reveal a departure from program implementation guidelines. For example, human resources are an important component of the program; at least four individuals are needed to effectively execute the elements of the program in a reading room. Schools implementing the program have to operate from the perspective of putting children first and utilizing their resources in ways that will promote learning for all students. In some instances, this has meant a reallocation of paraprofessionals to EOL classrooms to provide services to the lowest performing students. The leadership and staff have to work in collaboration to make such changes. They have to understand that students are increasingly placed at risk for failure when they reach third grade and are labeled as struggling readers and, in some cases, nonreaders. The EOL process underscores the need for schools to galvanize their resources to give all students, including their poorest readers, a fair chance for success.

CONCLUSION

The educational landscape in this country is witnessing a burgeoning of programs and practices, most of which are aimed at fulfilling many of what some call the threatening expectations laid out in the No Child Left Behind legislation. Educators are particularly concerned about being negatively categorized as not meeting adequate yearly progress. Unfortunately, though many are changing practices and working hard to fulfill those mandates, many children are being left behind. Until every child in every school learns to read, especially if they are not identified as having any cognitive challenges, they are still at risk of being left behind. That is because being able to read is such a basic necessity for being able to survive and contribute positively to society. When effectively implemented, the EOL process—though neither a quick fix nor a magic cure—is making a difference for numerous students, not just in terms of their reading achievement, but in terms of their holistic development.

Davis Street school demonstrates the results that are attainable when the leadership of a school works in collaboration with the rest of the staff, parents, and others in the school community to truly put children first. Long before the No Child Left Behind mandate, the staff at Davis were dedicated in their efforts to prevent any child from falling through the cracks. For them, EOL represented a unique opportunity to achieve that objective, from its pilot project to its continued implementation at that school and throughout the district. One of the core principles of the EOL program that is particularly emphasized in the reading room at Davis is that "every day at every station, every child must experience some success." They further believe—and have demonstrated—that students do not need to be fixed; very often, environments need to be changed to meet the needs of students in ways that will ensure their success.

References

Adams, M. (1991). *Beginning to read: Thinking and learning about print.* Cambridge, MA: MIT.

Beaver, J. (1997). *Developmental reading assessment resource guide.* Glenview, IL: Celebration.

Beck, I. L., & Juel, C. (1995). The role of decoding in learning to read. *American Educator, 19*(2), 21–25, 39–52.

Beers, K. (1998). Choosing not to read: Understanding why some middle schoolers just say no. In K. Beers & B. Samuels (Eds.), *Into Focus: Understanding and creating middle school readers* (pp. 81–104). Norwood, MA: Christopher-Gordon.

Beers, K. (2003). *When kids can't read: What teachers can do.* Portsmouth, NH: Heinemann.

Brown, F. (2004). Turning non-readers into readers through Essentials of Literacy. In E. T. Joyner, M. Ben-Avie, & J. P. Comer (Eds.), *Dynamic instructional leadership to support student learning and development* (pp. 177–187). Thousand Oaks, CA: Corwin.

Brown, F. E., Maholmes, V., Murray, E., & Nathan, L. (1998). Davis Street Magnet School: Linking child development with literacy. *Journal of Education for Students Placed At Risk, 31,* 23–38.

Cornwall, A., & Bawden, H. (1992). Reading disabilities and aggression: A critical review. *Journal of Learning Disabilities, 25,* 281–288.

Grosso De León, A. (2002). Moving beyond storybooks: Teaching our children to read to learn. *Carnegie Reporter, 2*(Fall), 3–11.

Fletcher, J., Shaywitz, S., Shakweiler, D., Katz, L., Liberman, I., Stuebing, K., et al. (1994). Cognitive profiles of reading disability: Comparisons of discrepancy and low achievement definitions. *Journal of Educational Psychology, 86,* 6–23.

Goodman, K. (1986). *What's whole in whole language?* Portsmouth, NH: Heinemann.

Hart, B., & Risley, T. (2003). The early catastrophe: The 30 million word gap by age 3. *American Educator, Spring,* 4–9.

Hill, M. (1998). Reaching struggling readers. In K. Beers & B. Samuels (Eds.), *Into Focus: Understanding and creating middle school readers* (pp. 81–104). Norwood, MA: Christopher-Gordon.

RAND Reading Study Group. (2002). *Reading for understanding: Toward an R & D program in reading comprehension.* Report prepared for the Office of Education Research and Improvement (OERI), Washington, DC. Washington, DC: OERI.

Shaywitz, S. (2003). *Overcoming dyslexia: A new and complete science-based program for reading problems at any level.* New York: Random House.

Shaywitz, S., Escobar, M., Shaywitz, B., Fletcher, J., & Makuch, R. (1992). Evidence that dyslexia may represent the lower tail of a normal distribution of reading disability. *New England Journal of Medicine, 326,* 145–150.

Slavin, R. (1998). Can education reduce social inequity? *Educational Leadership, 55,* 6–10.

Stanovich, K., & Siegel, L. (1994). Phenotypic performance profile of children with reading disabilities: A regression-based test of the phonological-core variable-difference model. *Journal of Educational Psychology, 86,* 24–53.

Werner, E. (1993). Risk, resilience, and recovery: Perspectives from the Kauai longitudinal study. *Development and Psychopathology, 5,* 503–515.

JOURNAL OF EDUCATION FOR STUDENTS PLACED AT RISK, *10*(2), 199–206

Maintaining Excellence While Managing Transitions: Norman S. Weir Revisited

Christine L. Emmons
Yale University Child Study Center

Ruth Baskerville
Norman S. Weir Elementary School
Paterson, New Jersey

In a national education climate where change is the only constant, Norman S. Weir Elementary School has maintained and expanded the reform efforts that have resulted in striking academic achievement and improved school climate. Despite changes in administration and staffing, a highly professional and committed staff has continued the implementation of the Comer School Development Program and sustained Weir as an outstanding intellectual and social development learning community.

NORMAN S. WEIR TODAY

The story of Norman S. Weir's [NSW] rise from one of the lowest performing to one of the highest performing schools in Paterson School District in New Jersey was told in a 1998 issue of the *Journal of Education for Students Placed at Risk*. That article (Emmons, Efimba, & Hagopian, 1998) covered the period from 1991 to 1996 and described the transformation of the school with the help of the Comer School Development Program. This article deals with 1998–2004, mainly from the point of view of the principal and members of the School Leadership Team. In the previous article (Emmons et al., 1998), we described the rise of Norman S. Weir from one of the lowest to one of the highest achieving schools in Paterson. In 1991, as one of the four lowest performing schools in Paterson, Norman S. Weir was directed by the superintendent to restructure to improve climate and student achieve-

Requests for reprints should be sent to Christine L. Emmons, School Development Program, Yale University Child Study Center, 55 College Street, New Haven, CT 06510–3208. E-mail: christine.emmons@yale.edu

ment. To comply with the directive, Norman S. Weir chose to work with the Advocacy Design Center Schools out of Columbia University Teachers College, through which they chose the Comer School Development Program (SDP) as the means of improving climate and student achievement.

By 1996, Norman S. Weir was one of the highest achieving schools in the district and the school climate had improved significantly. In 1994, when implementation of the Comer SDP began in earnest, no eighth grader at Norman S. Weir was at the highest level (Level 1) of competence in reading on New Jersey's Early Warning Tests. In 1996, 45.5% of Norman S. Weir's eighth graders attained Level 1 competence in reading. Similarly for mathematics, in 1994 no eighth grader at Weir was at Level 1 competence. In 1996, 18.2% of eighth graders at Weir attained Level 1 competence in mathematics, surpassing the district average of 10.3%.

The school climate improved from one of low staff morale and student disaffection with the learning process to one where staff members were "enthusiastic about their work, eager to collaborate with one another for the purpose of the development of their students, and willing to engage parents in partnership in the education process" (Emmons et al., 1998, p. 39). Students displayed higher self-esteem, greater belief in themselves, and an eagerness to learn. Both students and staff experienced a greater sense of belonging in an environment where staff worked collaboratively as they focused on fostering a climate defined by caring and strong academics.

This article describes the current reality of Norman S. Weir Elementary School. The consensus of the principal and 15 staff who responded to the *Norman S. Weir Elementary School Questionnaire* is that life at Norman S. Weir has been enjoyable and productive, even "wonderful." The student population has remained more or less the same in terms of demographics, but it has grown in size. Academic achievement remains high. The greatest change noted from the 1998 to 2004 period has been in staffing. There have been several retirements and new hires, as well as some transfers. Through all of the staff changes, the school has maintained its focus on the well-being of its students. The Comer facilitator writes,

Norman S. Weir's school climate is continuously reviewed and remediated. Teachers continually assess their delivery of instruction and adapt accordingly. The beauty of this building is that it is always striving for excellence.

Norman S. Weir, which includes Grades 1 through 8, has 300 students who are 46% Black, 48% Latino, 1% Asian, 4% White, and 1% "Other." There is still one general education class per grade. The student body is composed of general education students, cognitively impaired students, multiply disabled, language learning disabled, and deaf students. Some 90% of students receive free or reduced-price lunch. The average class size is 24 for general education and 11 for special education. The length of the school day is 6 hr 35 min with 5 hr 50 min spent in instructional time. The teacher–student ratio is 1:25 for general education, with the exception of reading and math. The special education population has a ratio of 1:12. The average attendance rate over the past 5 years has been 94%. The school's 2002–2003 report card (New Jersey Department of Education, 2003) lists English as the first language spoken in the home of all of Weir's students, and the overall faculty–student ratio as 1:6.7. In this report, 45% of Weir students are classified as Students with Disabilities requiring Individualized Education Programs (IEPs).

The general education student population continues to be drawn from a waiting list on a first-come, first-served basis. However, students with siblings already in the school are selected first. Students must apply for entry into the school, and the District Central Office assigns special education students to the school. Because Norman S. Weir is located in downtown Paterson, it has no neighborhood from which to draw students. The consensus is that there has been no significant change in the physical community in which the school is located, but one person pointed out that there has been growth in the downtown areas, with several new buildings, overcrowded parking, and a new preschool. The school is also surrounded by a community college.

Generally, the Comer Process is working well at Norman S. Weir. There is a sense of ownership of both successes and failures and a realization that the school community itself must make change happen. The Comer Process has helped staff to work better together and to view themselves as a cohesive group. As with all organic processes, continued vigilance is needed for progress to continue.

DATA SOURCES

The major sources of information for this article are the responses to the *Norman S. Weir Elementary School Questionnaire*, completed by the principal and about 15 staff members in September 2004, the Norman S. Weir 2002–2003 School Report Card, and the School Development Program (SDP) database of Leadership Academy Attendees. Six-year (1998–1999 to 2003–2004) attendance and achievement trend data were obtained from Principal Baskerville. Notes from a June 2004 site visit of an implementation coordinator provided additional information.

MANAGING TRANSITIONS

Staff Development and Support

In 1997, Dr. Hagopian[1] was assigned to the New Jersey Department of Education and Dr. Ruth Baskerville was appointed principal of Norman S. Weir. Unlike what

---

[1]Dr. Hagopian died in 2001. We honor her for her dedication to children.

many principals do on assuming command, Principal Baskerville decided to continue processes that were working well in the school. As such, she continued the use of the Comer SDP and deepened implementation by embarking on a program of staff development in the Comer Process. In October 1998, Principal Baskerville and a team of nine staff members from Norman S. Weir attended the Comer SDP 101 Leadership Academy. This team included the chairpersons of the School Leadership Council, the Student and Staff Support Team, the Parent Team, the Comer facilitator, a social worker, and teachers. In January 1999, Principal Baskerville returned with this team to attend the Comer SDP 102 Leadership Academy. This action ensured that key people involved in the implementation of the Comer Process would have the knowledge and skills to further enhance the process.

Staff development in the Comer Process has continued over the years with additional staff (as well as members of the original team), parents, and students attending various Comer SDP Leadership Academies. For example, Principal Baskerville and five staff members (four from the original group of nine) participated in the Comer SDP Summer Policy Institute in Washington, DC, in July 1999; 10 students, 3 parents, and 1 staff member attended the Comer Kids' Academy in July 2002. (The Comer Kids' Academy takes place in conjunction with the Principals' Academy.) Principal Baskerville served as one of the Principals in Residence at the Principals' Academy in 2002.

As with all schools implementing the Comer SDP, an Implementation Coordinator was assigned to Norman S. Weir to help shepherd the process. The Implementation Coordinator is a Comer SDP staff member who visits the school several times a year to work with the Comer School Facilitator and the School Leadership Council, providing on-site consultation and staff development as needed.

Implementation of the Comer Process

As a result of continuous staff development and support, the Comer Process is working well at Norman S. Weir. According to Principal Baskerville, the School Planning and Management Team, now called the School Leadership Council (SLC), "has worked exceptionally well, meeting regularly [twice a month] to manage every aspect of school life." Staff feel that the SLC is "very efficient and runs effectively," "has been a driving force in making improvements," and is a "model for shared decision making." One staff member shared the opinion that the SLC may need to make a greater effort to involve staff who are not SLC members or who do not regularly attend SLC meetings.

The SLC maintains ongoing minutes, agendas, and Process Observer's comments. Some of the major issues addressed have been staffing, school repairs, special events, and budgets. Due to the effectiveness of the SLC, the school got new air conditioning and heating units after much discussion with the Central Office. The school was able to keep its carnival when the budget became too small to sustain it throughout the district. The SLC has also helped the school to get grants for various activities and programs, worked to get the building upgraded to state standards, addressed class size, and suggested workshops to be presented. The SLC is spearheading the drive for Norman S. Weir to become a true community school with medical, dental, and health services on site. The SLC has developed new community liaisons that are helping the school to meet this goal.

The Student and Staff Support Team (SSST), which has addressed a range of issues dealing with students' academic and social needs, student attendance, tardiness, and discipline, has functioned well and been effective. The SSST has maintained minutes, agendas, and Process Observer's comments for each meeting. The SSST organizes an annual Health Fair with much joint parent and staff participation. Other major issues addressed are "the need for more involvement with the community via a community resource fair" and "fire drill procedures." One area for improvement identified by a staff member is dissemination of information regarding their activities.

Although the Parent Team has contributed to the improvement of the school community by helping with the development of the Comprehensive School Plan that addresses all school issues, holding successful fundraisers, purchasing and distributing planners, and assisting in other ways, the adequate functioning of the Parent Team appears to be a challenge. Staff members do not perceive it as functioning as well or as consistently as the SLC and SSST, although Principal Baskerville views the Parent Team as having functioned satisfactorily until the 2003–2004 school year. Personal problems of three of the four officers during the 2003–2004 school year affected the functioning of the Team. In the summer of 2004, those three officers resigned.

In addition to the three Comer Teams, Norman S. Weir has several committees: Fundraising, Public Relations, Curriculum and Grant, School Climate, and Staff Development.

The Comer SDP guiding principles of collaboration, consensus decision making, and no-fault problem solving continue to be practiced at Norman S. Weir. These principles are used at all meetings. Collaboration is practiced daily at all levels, including general education classes. Decisions are reached through consensus at all meetings and no-fault problem solving is routinely practiced, but this does not mean that the principal does not hold everyone accountable.

Staff development over the past 5 years has focused on collaborative teaching, inclusion, and student management. These staff development activities have resulted in better behaved students with better time-on-task instruction.

Academic Programs

The two major staff development initiatives implemented in the school during the principalship of Dr. Hagopian (1994–1995 to 1996–1997)—the collaborative in-class model and the computer and Internet competency training—have remained in place and expanded with visible results. New staff members are trained in the collaborative in-class model as they come on board. All students have computer classes weekly and staff competency in computer use has grown to such an extent that they have created their plan book and gradebook formats from the Internet. The Norman S. Weir 2002–2003 School Report Card shows that the computer–student ratio has improved from 1:8.7 in 2000–2001 to 1:3.6 in 2002–2003, surpassing the state average of 1:4.4. The state average in 2000–2001 was 1: 5.2. The 2002–2003 also shows that 100% of Weir's classrooms and library–media centers have been wired for Internet connectivity since 2000–2001.

The practice of having students remain with the same math teacher, reading teacher, and language teacher for 3 years from sixth to eighth grade is still in place and is working very well. Principal Baskerville credits it as one of the strongest reasons for the academic success of their students. She emphasizes that teachers get to know the students and their parents very well. Algebra I continues to be offered to students for credit. It is taught from 7:15 to 8:00 a.m. daily.

Additional activities that directly target the improvement of academic achievement are cluster meetings, after-school programs, and the pacing of the curricula.

STUDENT ACHIEVEMENT

Over the years, Weir has maintained high academic achievement even through changes in administration and tests. As noted earlier, in 1997, Dr. Hagopian was assigned to the New Jersey Department of Education Office and Dr. Ruth Baskerville was appointed principal of Norman S. Weir. In the 2002–2003 school year, the New Jersey Assessment of Skills and Knowledge (NJASK4) for fourth graders replaced the Elementary School Proficiency Assessment (ESPA). In that year, 95.9% of Weir fourth graders achieved full or advanced proficiency on the NJASK4 Language Arts Literacy as compared to 52.9% of fourth graders for the Paterson District and 77.6% of fourth graders statewide. Similarly, 95.9% of Weir fourth graders achieved full or advanced proficiency on NJASK4 Mathematics as compared to 43.2% the Paterson District fourth graders and 68.0% of New Jersey fourth graders.

In the past school year, 2003–2004, 100% of Norman S. Weir fourth graders achieved full or advanced proficiency on the NJASK4 Mathematics and on the NJASK4 Language Arts Proficiency. Among the eighth graders at Weir, 76.9% achieved full or advanced proficiency in Language Arts, 53.8% achieved full or advanced proficiency in Mathematics, and 80.8% achieved full or advanced proficiency in Science on the Grade Eight Proficiency Assessment.

SCHOOL CLIMATE

The consensus is that school climate remains positive and spirited, with high academic achievement for students. Staff members describe the social climate as "relaxed and professional," "very good," "terrific," and "great." Only one person wrote, "needs to be worked on." The quality of the interpersonal relationships was emphasized. One person writes, "The relationship among teachers is fantastic even though there's been a large number of teachers hired over the past couple of years." Another states, "I can only tell you about myself. I feel that I have excellent working relationships with other teachers, parents, and students. Personality of staff has a large impact on these relationships." A final quote sums up the feeling at Norman S. Weir: "At NSW we take relationships seriously. ... Every staff member is valued. Every student is valued. Every parent is valued."

Principal Baskerville notes that relationships among students, staff, and parents are strong and that she never allows anyone to mistreat another. She requires parents, staff, and students to follow proper deportment etiquette and expects teachers to share materials freely. General and special education staff are comfortable mainstreaming students. One staff member considers it significant that parents stand in line to apply to get their children into the school.

PARENT INVOLVEMENT

Parents are involved in many ways in the life of the school. In addition to the 24 regular members of the Parent Team, one or two parents sit on each of the other SDP teams and school committees. Parents also participate by getting their children to the school and by ensuring that they do their homework. Parents also help teachers in some of the classrooms, especially the lower grades, and serve as chaperones on field trips. Parents are also very involved in the school carnival. School events are generally well attended by parents.

The school attempts to promote parent involvement through publicity and special evening and weekend programs. Parents are encouraged to serve on committees and each parent signs a contract at the beginning of the school year. There is an open-door policy for parents and surveys are conducted every year to solicit their input. Teachers also call parents at home and send memos in an effort to get parents more involved.

LOOKING TO THE FUTURE

The school community is looking forward to the school's becoming a true community school within 5 years, with medical, dental, and health services on site. This is a major goal of the SLC, which is partnering with community organizations to achieve this goal. Staff understand that it will take training, joint fund raising with community organizations, and patience to achieve their goal, but they are excited about the prospect of reaching this level of service to students.

CONCLUSION

When asked what they would like the world to know about their school, staff members wrote the following, a selection of direct quotes taken from their responses to the questionnaire:

> [Norman S. Weir Elementary School] is a caring, highly academic institution where [they] carefully monitor progress, disaggregate test data, and have fun while building character! [It] is a wonderful place to work and study. The staff are very well educated and know how to get their students motivated and willing to learn. Dedication is the key at NSW. When new programs are introduced, NSW is among the first to show interest and jump on the bandwagon.
>
> Our school ... is scoring higher than the mean [of] suburban schools on our state tests. [It] has dedicated teachers and follows an excellent whole-school reform model that has made a positive impact on students' academics, as well as their whole psychological beings. This impact applies to staff and parents as well. We believe all children can learn through a disciplined environment full of high expectations and a loving staff to support them. We are doing our best to make this school the best one in Paterson.
>
> Norman is a wonderful school to work for. We have the best staff [who] will go the extra miles to do what is in the best interest of children. Our parents come when called upon. We are a successful school which embraces change.

POSTSCRIPT

In June 2004, seven key staff members retired, and Principal Baskerville retired on November 1, 2004. To ensure continuity, they have already brought new staff into the "Comer fold."

REFERENCES

Emmons, C. L., Efimba, M. O., & Hagopian, G. (1998). A school transformed: The case of Norman S. Weir. *Journal of Education for Students Placed At Risk, 3,* 39–51.

New Jersey Department of Education. (2003). *Norman S. Weir 2002–2003 school report card.* Retrieved from http://education.state.nj.us/rc/rc03/letter.html

JOURNAL OF EDUCATION FOR STUDENTS PLACED AT RISK, *10*(2), 207–224

Extending Opportunity to Learn for Students Placed At Risk

Pamela S. Nesselrodt
Education Department
Dickinson College

Christianna L. Alger
School of Teacher Education
San Diego State University

This article describes a viable alternative to hiring full-time certified teachers or to using lay volunteers to provide children at risk of failing in school with academic coaches (tutors). The *Academic Coaching Program* described herein recruited and trained students enrolled in a university's school of education programs to serve as academic coaches primarily for 7th and 8th graders in an inner-city school in which 96% of the students are placed at risk by the socioeconomic (SES) status of their families. The program extended the school's regular instructional programs in reading and mathematics. It provided the at-risk students with high-quality coaching by university students through a systematic process of training the university students in the school's reading and mathematics programs, monitoring them as they coached, and providing feedback to the coaches on a regular basis.

Located in inner-city Chicago, Silverstein Elementary School[1] has a student population in which over 96% are placed at risk for failure in school because of the socioeconomic status (SES) of their families. All of the 715 children are minorities. Since 1983, the Pre-K/Grade 8 school has been committed to equality of opportunity to learn for its students through the implementation of Mortimer Adler's *Paideia Proposal* (1982). The Paideia program is based on Adler's concept of how children should be educated in a democratic society. Adler espoused the idea that all children are entitled to the same quality of education. As he described it, all

---

Requests for reprints should be sent to Pamela S. Nesselrodt, Education Department, Dickinson College, P.O. Box 1773, Carlisle, PA 17013. E-mail: nesselrp@dickinson.edu

[1]For confidentiality reasons, the name of the school has been changed.

children should be given "cream" rather than some being given "cream" while others are given "skim milk." The program seeks to develop all aspects of the students' cognitions: "acquisition of knowledge, development of intellectual skills, and enlarged understanding of ideas and values" (Adler, 1984, p. 8). It does so by providing a curriculum framework that defines goals, means to those goals, and areas, operations, and activities related to these means and goals. The program also makes curricular suggestions based primarily on "great" pieces of western literature and conceptual understanding along with three instructional methods: didactic instruction, coaching, and maieutic or Socratic questioning. Finally, the program argues for the necessity of providing children with high and clearly communicated expectations for not only their academic success but appropriate "deportment" as well (Adler, 1982, pp. 55–56).

In 1993, Silverstein Elementary School began to strengthen its Paideia program by focusing on improving the children's reading and mathematics skills through the integration into its Paideia program of the highly scripted and controversial Direct Instruction program. Direct Instruction, developed at the University of Oregon, meets the demands of Adler's description of the didactic mode of teaching and, to some degree, the coaching mode as well. The coaching mode of teaching has, in fact, been the most difficult for Paideia schools all over the United States to implement because it requires that children receive individual attention from their teachers to help them in the building of skills, whether these be in reading, mathematics, or other subjects. Some schools have hired full-time coaches to fulfill that role with their students. Others have relied on computers and forms of cooperative learning in which children coach each other.

There is a good bit of research that suggests that the most effective teaching is that in which a learner is paired with an individual tutor who coaches the learner during the development of academic skills (Wasik & Slavin, 1993). However, the expense and logistics of public education in the United States usually prohibit this kind of instruction. Therefore, a viable alternative to providing an individual, certified teacher for each learner enrolled in a school is to provide those children with the greatest needs with tutors or academic coaches.

To provide this kind of focused academic coaching, the Chicago Public Schools initiated the 10,000 Tutors grant program in 1996. The program funded tutoring initiatives designed and implemented by local universities as well as civic and church groups. The lead author of this article, then on the faculty of Loyola University Chicago, was awarded a series of these grants to provide tutoring services to children at Silverstein School during the 1996–1997, 1997–1998, and 1998–1999 academic years. The Academic Coaching Program, as it was called, provided coaching by university students from the school of education to (primarily) seventh and eighth graders who showed the greatest need for focused, adult instructional attention. This program ensured high-quality coaching by the university students through a systematic process of training them in the reading and mathematics programs used at Silverstein, monitoring them as they coached, and providing feedback to the coaches on a regular basis. It also provided the children at Silverstein with a consistent schedule of coaching to compensate for the likely lack of academic support at home. The Academic Coaching Program, then, provided high-quality, small-group instruction for Silverstein students that was closely linked to their regular instructional program. By utilizing university students pursuing careers in education or other human services, the cost was much lower than hiring full-time certified teachers to coach children.

RELATED LITERATURE

The need for extra assistance for at-risk middle-grade students in both reading and mathematics is stressed by Balfanz, Ruby, and Mac Iver (2002). They asserted that students entering high-poverty middle schools generally test 2 or more years below grade level in both reading and math. They also indicate that these students "enter with different 'pockets of knowledge,'" which requires a more individualized approach to provide them with meaningful instructional assistance (p. 137). Balfanz et al. (2002) found that after-school and Saturday programs generally provide sporadic assistance to at-risk middle-grade students because of their poor attendance and "a mix of high and low quality instruction, which may or may not be in the areas where a given student needs extra help" (p. 138). They believed that a more effective approach to this problem is "to offer sustained, systematic, and differentiated high quality extra help ... *during the school day*" that is "both supplemental and linked to the student's regular classroom instruction" (p. 139).

In describing the importance of providing academic coaching to learners, Adler (1982) stated that "the development of the intellectual skills" requires that "one must not only engage in doing them, but one must be guided in doing them by someone more expert in doing them than oneself" (p. 52). He further described this "coaching" as necessarily being done either individually or in small groups, "if the groups are small enough to allow the coach to give individual attention where it is needed" (p. 52). In responding to questions about the implementation of the Paideia Proposal, Adler (1983) stated, "The coaching of intellectual skills cannot be done well with a ratio of more than ten to one; it will be better done when the ratio is larger—nearer five or six to one" (p. 61). In describing the importance of coaching to the improvement of language skills, Geraldine Van Doren (1984) asserted, "Coaching lies at the heart of the language program" (p. 61). She further advised that "additional coaching must be available through the program for students who need it to keep from falling behind" (p. 62). Likewise, Charles Van Doren (1984, p. 76) stressed the importance of guided practice in learning mathematics.

Slavin (2002) described "one-to-one adult-to-child tutoring" as "one of the most effective instructional strategies known" (p. 307). He conceded, however, that it is also a costly proposition. He suggested using adult volunteers such as college students to provide low-cost academic coaching. Fitzgerald (2001) also found that college students with minimal training in tutoring methodologies provided effective academic assistance for at-risk learners at a cost substantially lower than hiring fully certified teachers as tutors. Results of the Stetson Reads Project suggest that "in order to enhance the effectiveness of [tutoring] programs," program implementers should recruit education majors to serve in tutoring programs rather than a more general population of college students because they already have some training in pedagogy (Heins, Perry, & Piechura-Couture, 1999, p. 118). Tingley (2001) and Wasik (1997) found that supervision and well-structured materials are essential in effectively using volunteer tutors.

Finally, the affective element of the tutor–tutee relationship was explored by Shumow (2001) and Cobb (1998). Shumow (2001) indicated that "a positive emotional climate ... should increase attendance" and, therefore, the effectiveness of the tutoring program, particularly with older at-risk learners (p. 4). Cobb (1998) found that "highly successful tutors" in her program formed a positive bond with the older at-risk learners who participated (p. 11).

PURPOSE

Because Silverstein was particularly interested in improving the achievement of its students on the Iowa Test of Basic Skills, the effectiveness of the Academic Coaching Program was measured by the gain scores of the at-risk students on that battery of standardized tests for each of the 3 years of the program. In addition, during Years 2 and 3, an attitude scale was developed and administered to the students to determine their affective responses to various aspects of the program. This article presents and discusses the results of these evaluations.

PROGRAM DESCRIPTION

As described earlier, the primary purpose of the Academic Coaching Program was to provide at-risk seventh and eighth graders in an inner-city school with a consistent schedule of academic assistance that was closely linked to the school's programs. In addition, it provided preservice teacher education students enrolled in the university's teacher preparation program with an opportunity to work with children placed at risk by their home environments. It also gave these teacher education students a chance to develop their teaching skills. This article focuses on the effects of the program on the seventh and eighth graders' achievement in reading and mathematics as measured by the Iowa Test of Basic Skills. This battery of tests was administered by the school district annually to all students and used at several benchmark years to determine whether students would be retained or promoted to the next grade. The eighth grade was one of those benchmark years. The Academic Coaching Program extended the school's regular reading instruction by reinforcing word attack skills, comprehension skills, and vocabulary skills that were emphasized in the school's reading program. It also extended the school's regular mathematics program by focusing on computation and problem-solving skills emphasized in the school's math program. During Years 1 and 2 of the program, these skills were supplemented with sessions designed to enhance the students' test-taking strategies that would prove useful in taking standardized tests.

Selection of At-Risk Students

Students enrolled in the program were primarily seventh and eighth graders, along with a few sixth graders who had been identified by their teachers and the school's administrative team as being in the most need of academic assistance. This determination was based on the children's achievement on previously administered standardized tests and their achievement in class. The number of children served each year ranged from 35 to 50, depending on the number of available coaches as well as the number of students interested in participating in the program. During Years 1 and 2 of the program, students' attendance was closely monitored by the school's assistant principal to determine whether students were taking advantage of the opportunity for additional instructional assistance for approximately the first 2 weeks of the program. Students who were absent on 2 consecutive sessions were pulled from the program and replaced with other selected students. Over the 3-year period, the coach-to-student ratio ranged from 1:4 to 1:7 depending on the number of children recommended for services and the number of available coaches.

Selection of Academic Coaches

Each semester of the 3 years, between 8 and 13 academic coaches (tutors) were selected by the authors of this article, a teacher educator and her graduate assistant, who coordinated the program. The coaches were recruited primarily from students enrolled in Loyola University Chicago's teacher preparation program. Recruiting was conducted by visits to classes in the teacher education program during which information about the program was provided. Preservice teachers were invited to apply for selection into the program. Applicants indicated the program in which they were enrolled as well as their level within the program, their grade point averages, a statement of why they would like to participate in the program, and names of references. The applications were reviewed and coaches with strong academic backgrounds and appropriate recommendations were selected to participate. The coaches either were paid $10 per hour for their services or used their hours in partial fulfillment of state requirements for 100 hr of field experiences prior to student teaching.

Schedule of Coaching Sessions

During the 3-year period, three different schedules were tried. The 1996–1997 academic year saw the coaching sessions scheduled before school from 8 a.m. to 9 a.m. on Mondays, Wednesdays, and Fridays. Fall sessions began in early October and lasted through late November with a total of 20 sessions. Spring sessions began in early February and ran through mid-April with a total of 26 sessions.

An evaluation of the attendance of the at-risk students at sessions held before school led to a change in the schedule during the 1997–1998 academic year. The sessions were scheduled on Mondays, Wednesdays, and Fridays from 1 p.m. to 2 p.m., which was near the end of the school day. This change was implemented to improve attendance and thus maximize the available time during which the children would be provided with more individualized instruction than could be provided in a classroom with 27 students. Fall sessions began in late September and ran through late November with a total of 22 sessions. Spring sessions began in early February and ran through early April with a total of 16 sessions.

Experiences from the 1996–1997 and 1997–1998 academic years indicated that attendance of both at-risk students and academic coaches was better when the sessions were held in the afternoon. However, because the 1 p.m.–2 p.m. schedule shortened instructional time for the children within their regular classes, it was determined that the sessions should begin near the end of the school day and extend until slightly after school. During the 1998–1999 academic year, services were provided on Mondays, Wednesdays, and Fridays between 1:45 p.m. and 2:45 p.m. Fall sessions began in early October and ran through early December with a total of 20 sessions. Spring sessions began in late February and ran through early May with a total of 20 sessions.

Focus of Coaching Sessions

As described previously, the overall focus of the coaching sessions was the improvement of the at-risk students' skills in reading and mathematics, as well as strengthening their test-taking strategies. However, as with the scheduling of the coaching sessions, the particular instructional methodologies and materials used changed each year to better accommodate the needs of the children as defined by school personnel. In general, the coaching sessions focused primarily on reading during the fall semesters and mathematics during the spring semesters.

During the Fall 1996 coaching sessions, all but one of the coaches used a whole-language reading series with the children as a complement to the school's Direction Instruction program. Children worked on reading comprehension and vocabulary building within the context of the stories contained in the series. The coach who did not use the whole-language series was working with a group of eighth graders who had been retained because of unacceptable scores on the Iowa Test of Basic Skills. She used materials provided by the school district that focused on reading in the various content areas. Skill areas focused on with all participants in the program included the following: contextual meaning of words, drawing conclusions, viewpoint, making predictions, and cause and effect.

During the Spring 1997 sessions, academic coaches focused on improving the reading, mathematics, and test-taking skills of the at-risk students. They did this primarily by working with the children on practice tests with a format similar to the Iowa Test of Basic Skills. The areas focused on in reading included contextual meaning of words, drawing conclusions, viewpoint, making predictions, and cause and effect. Areas of focus in mathematics included geometry, basic calculations, measurements, and basic algebra. In addition to this, one tutor majoring in mathematics worked with a group of children on Tuesday and Thursday mornings primarily in mathematics. Another worked with a group of children who needed enrichment activities by reading and discussing novels with them.

Fall 1997 saw the academic coaches again focusing on improving the reading skills of the at-risk students using materials developed by the school district for use in their summer "bridge" program. The summer program was a remedial program provided for children throughout the district who had not achieved acceptable Iowa Test scores at the benchmark years to warrant their promotion to the next grade. In addition to these district-developed materials, the coaches worked with the at-risk students in their reading of two novels, which were studied in small groups. As during the previous year, the areas of focus in reading included contextual meaning of words, drawing conclusions, viewpoint, making predictions, and cause and effect.

Spring 1998 saw the academic coaches again focusing on improving the mathematics skills of the at-risk seventh and eighth graders. This time, however, they used materials developed for a televised program called *Countdown* (Schiller, Giroux, Gozan, & Thomas, 1991–2002). This program was developed around areas of mathematics targeted in the Iowa Test of Basic Skills. Areas of focus in mathematics included geometry, statistical reasoning, and basic algebra.

As with the previous two fall semesters, the Fall 1998 sessions focused on improving the reading skills of the at-risk children. In an effort to refocus attention on the Socratic methodologies of the school's Paideia program, the bases for the instruction were selections that were to be discussed in the weekly seminars held in each classroom. The children's teachers chose the selections to be used as the bases of their work. The coaches used Reciprocal Teaching (Palincsar & Brown, 1984) methodology to again focus on contextual meaning of words, drawing conclusions, viewpoint, making predictions, and cause and effect.

As during previous spring semesters, coaches focused on the improvement of the children's math skills in geometry, statistical reasoning, and basic algebra. As during the Spring 1998 semester, they used the *Countdown* materials. The decision was made this time, however, not to use test materials similar to the Iowa Test of *Basic Skills* to enhance the students' test-taking skills because the children quickly became bored with them.

Training and Supervision of Academic Coaches

In general, training of the academic coaches was a coordinated effort of school personnel and the authors of this article, who coordinated the Academic Coaching Program. The training schedule and content varied each semester depending on the materials being used and available time as well as ongoing evaluation of the training by the program coordinators. Each semester, Silverstein personnel introduced the coaches to the instructional programs of the school. If materials provided by the school were to be used by the coaches, school personnel conducted training sessions for the coaches in the use of the materials both by describing their use and modeling the use of the materials with them. If materials and methodologies were provided by the university, university personnel conducted the training sessions, again by describing their use and modeling the use of methods and materials with the coaches. This formal training was for 1.5 hr sessions during a 2- to 3-day period at the beginning of each semester totaling from 3 to 4.5 hr each semester. Most semesters provided an additional training session about halfway through to further refine the coaches' tutoring skills.

In addition to these formal training sessions, the coaches were supervised by one of the university coordinators during each coaching session. This entailed observing individual tutors and their interactions with the at-risk students and providing written feedback to each tutor each day. And, because the coaches and supervisors traveled together by van from the university's campus to Silverstein and back each day, the 60-min round-trip travel time was used for discussion among the coaches and supervisors aimed at improving the instruction being provided to the children. Summary sessions involving school personnel, coaches, and university personnel were also held at the end of each semester to discuss more and less effective aspects of the program.

Finally, coaches provided reports on the at-risk students' progress in the content being studied, their participation and attitude, overall performance, and attendance to school personnel and the parents/guardians of the children. Coaches were provided with training in writing commentary in each of the categories being assessed. Their reports were reviewed by university personnel prior to distribution to the school and parents/guardians. If comments were deemed inappropriate, university personnel worked with the coaches to modify them.

RESULTS

Because the school district relied primarily on grade equivalency scores on the Iowa Test of Basic Skills to measure the educational progress of its students, those scores were used as the primary outcome measures for the Academic Coaching Program for each of the 3 years of the program. T tests for paired samples were run using the grade equivalency scores to determine whether the gains from one year to the next for children participating in the program were statistically significant at the .000 level for both reading and math. *T* tests for independent samples were also run to determine whether the gains in the grade equivalency scores for those children participating in the program were statistically significantly different from those not participating in the program. Finally, during the 1997–1998 and 1998–1999 academic years, the attitudes of children participating in the program toward the program were assessed using a Tutoring Attitude Scale developed by the authors of this article (see the Appendix for a copy of this scale).

Scores for 40 children were used to evaluate the effect of the Academic Coaching Program on the reading portion of the Iowa Test of Basic Skills from 1996 to 1997. The mean of the paired differences was .9450 with a standard deviation of .808 and a *t* value of 7.40 with 39 *df*. This yielded a *p* value of .000. In math, scores for 32 students were used for the *t* test. The mean of the paired differences was .7656 with a standard deviation of .666 and a *t* value of 6.50 with 51 *df*. This yielded a *p* value of .000.

T tests for independent samples were used to determine whether the gains in grade equivalency scores from 1996 to 1997 of children participating in the program were significantly different from those not participating in the program and yielded no statistically significant difference in either reading or math. However, the mean improvement of the 40 children participating in the reading portion of the Academic Coaching Program was .9450, whereas the mean improvement of the 30 children receiving no assistance beyond their regular classroom instruction in Reading was .9200. This is a mean difference of .0250 in favor of those participating in the program. *T* tests run on math scores yielded similar results. The mean improvement of the 32 students receiving academic coaching in mathematics was .7656, whereas the mean improvement of the 30 students receiving no assistance beyond the school's regular program was .7400. This is a mean difference of .0256 in favor of those participating in the Academic Coaching Program.

From 1997 to 1998, scores for 35 students were used to evaluate the effect of the Academic Coaching Program on the reading portion of the Iowa Test of Basic Skills. The mean of the paired differences was .9514 with a standard deviation of .848 and a *t* value of 6.64 with 34 *df*. This yielded a *p* value of .000. In math, there were 35 students' scores used for the *t* test as well. The mean of the paired differences was .8000 with a standard deviation of .667 and a *t* value of 7.09 with 34 *df*. This yielded a *p* value of .000.

As in the previous year, *t* tests for independent samples were also run to determine whether the gains in the grade equivalency scores from 1997–1998 of children participating in the program were significantly different from those not participating in the program. Again, these tests yielded no statistically significant difference in either reading or math. However, as in the previous year, the mean improvement of the 35 children participating in the reading portion of the Academic

Coaching Program was greater than those receiving no assistance beyond their regular class instruction. The mean improvement score for those participating in the reading portion of the program was .9514, whereas the mean improvement of the 67 children receiving no assistance beyond the school's regular instruction in reading was .8030. This is a mean difference of .1484 in favor of those participating in the Academic Coaching Program. T tests run on math scores did not yield the same results. The mean improvement of the 35 students receiving coaching in mathematics was .8000, whereas the mean of the 67 children receiving no assistance beyond their regular program was .8104. This is a mean difference of .0104 in favor of those not participating in the Academic Coaching Program—a substantially smaller difference than the mean improvements in reading scores.

Finally, a t test for paired samples was run to determine whether the gains on the Iowa Test of Basic Skills from 1998 to 1999 for children participating in the program were statistically significant at the .000 level for both reading and math. In reading, there were 39 students whose scores were used. The mean of the paired differences was .6564 with a standard deviation of 1.104 and a t value of 3.713 with 38 df. This yielded a p value of .000. In math, there were 38 students' scores used for the t test. The mean of the paired differences was .9632 with a standard deviation of .5518 and a t value of 10.758 with 37 df. This yielded a p value of .000.

Again, t tests for independent samples were run to determine whether the gains in the grade equivalency scores from 1998–1999 of children participating in the program were significantly different from those not participating in the program. These tests yielded no statistically significant difference in either reading or math. The mean improvement of the 39 children participating in the reading portion of the Academic Coaching Program whose scores were analyzed was .6564, whereas the mean improvement of the 50 children receiving no assistance beyond their regular instruction in reading was .8960. This is a mean difference of .2396 in favor of those not participating in the Academic Coaching Program. T tests run on math scores yielded somewhat similar results. The mean improvement of the 38 students receiving coaching in mathematics whose scores were analyzed was .9632, whereas the mean of those 50 children receiving no assistance beyond the school's regular program was .9860. This is a mean difference of .0228 in favor of those not participating in the Academic Coaching Program—a substantially smaller difference than the mean improvements in reading scores.

Table 1 summarizes the results of t tests for paired samples for the 3 years of the program in reading. This indicates that children participating in the Academic Coaching Program showed statistically significant gains in their reading scores on the Iowa Test of Basic Skills for each of the 3 years. During Years 1 and 2 of the program, the mean difference remained fairly stable at .9450 and .9514, respectively. During the 3rd year, however, the mean difference was lower at .6564 but still statistically significant.

T tests for paired samples on math scores on the Iowa Test of Basic Skills for the 3 years of the Academic Coaching Program are summarized in Table 2. As in read-

TABLE 1
T Tests for Paired Samples in Reading With Academic Coaching Program

Cases	MD	SD	t	df	p
Year 1 (n = 40)	.9450	.808	7.40	39	.000
Year 2 (n = 35)	.9514	.848	6.64	34	.000
Year 3 (n = 39)	.6564	1.104	3.71	38	.000

TABLE 2
T Tests for Paired Samples in Math With Academic Coaching Program

Cases	MD	SD	t	df	p
Year 1 (n = 32)	.7656	.666	6.50	51	.000
Year 2 (n = 35)	.8000	.667	7.09	34	.000
Year 3 (n = 38)	.9632	.552	10.76	37	.000

ing, children participating in the program showed statistically significant gains in math for each of the 3 years with a steady increase in the mean differences during each of the 3 years. The mean difference for the 1st year was .7656. At the end of the 2nd year of the program, the mean difference in math achievement increased slightly to .8000, whereas the 3rd year saw a jump in the mean difference in math achievement to .9632.

T tests for independent samples in reading on the Iowa Test of Basic Skills are summarized in Table 3. The results of these t tests allow for a comparison of mean improvement scores of students who participated in the Academic Coaching Program with those who did not over the 3 years of the program. During Years 1 and 2 of the program, children who participated in the program demonstrated a mean improvement in reading scores of .9450 and .9514, respectively, whereas those who did not receive the service demonstrated a mean improvement in reading scores of .9200 and .8030, respectively. Thus, the children who participated in the program showed greater improvement in scores on reading on the Iowa Test of Basic Skills than those who did not participate in the program, with a mean differences of .0250 in the 1st year and .1484 in the 2nd year. During the 3rd year of the program, the

TABLE 3
T Tests for Independent Samples in Reading

Cases	MI With Coaching	MI Without Coaching	Mean Difference
Year 1	.9450 (n = 40)	.9200 (n = 30)	.0250
Year 2	.9514 (n = 35)	.8030 (n = 67)	.1484
Year 3	.6564 (n = 39)	.8960 (n = 50)	.2396

Note.   MI = mean improvement.

children who did not participate in the Academic Coaching Program showed a mean improvement on reading scores of .8960, whereas those who received the services of the program showed a mean improvement on reading scores of .6564. In this case, the mean difference in reading scores of the two groups of children was .2396, in favor of those not participating in the program.

Table 4 summarizes results of t tests for independent samples in math on the Iowa Test of Basic Skills. Mean improvement in math scores of children participating in the Academic Coaching Program increased each year from .7656 in the 1st year of the program, to .8000 in the 2nd year, to .9632 in the 3rd year. Likewise, the mean improvement in math scores of children not participating in the program increased from .7400 in the 1st year, to .8104 in the 2nd year, to .9860 in the 3rd year. During the 1st year of the program, the mean improvement in math scores of the children participating in the program was greater than the mean improvement in math scores of the children not participating in the program with a mean difference of .0256. During the 2nd and 3rd years, however, the mean improvement in math was greater for those not participating in the program with a mean difference of .0104 in the 2nd year and a mean difference of .0228 in the 3rd year.

Because learner's emotions and attitudes toward instruction, instructors, and the instructional setting have been shown to have a significant effect on their learning, the attitudes of the children participating in the Academic Coaching Program toward various aspects of the program were assessed during Years 2 and 3 of the program. This assessment was conducted using a Tutoring Attitude Scale developed by the authors of this article. The Tutoring Attitude Scale was modeled on the *Estes Attitude Scales* (Estes, n.d.), which measure students' attitudes toward various school subjects (see the Appendix for a copy of the Tutoring Attitude Scale).

During 1997–1998, 22 of the 35 children participating in the program responded to the survey. Overall the children's attitudes were positive. The analysis of the survey was completed by placing the questions into four categories: Curriculum and Instruction, Teacher (Coach) Characteristics, Student Characteristics, and Physical Setting. The responses for each question were tallied by category as well (Agree, Disagree, and Don't Know). Percentages were calculated for each response category for each question. Finally, total positive and negative responses for each of the four categories and overall percentages for positive and negative responses for each of the four categories were calculated. Seventy-nine percent of the responses were in agreement with positive statements pertaining to Curriculum and Instruction, whereas 37% of the responses were in agreement with negative statements pertaining to this category. Seventy-eight percent of the responses were in agreement with positive statements about Teacher (Coach) Characteristics, whereas 19% were in agreement with the only negative statement pertaining to this category. Sixty-four percent of the responses were in agreement with positive statements pertaining to Student Characteristics, whereas 25% were in agreement with negative statements pertaining to Student Characteristics. Responses to statements pertaining to the Physical Setting in which the tutoring took place were

TABLE 4
T Tests for Independent Samples in Math

Cases	MI With Coaching	MI Without Coaching	Mean Difference
Year 1	.7656 ($n = 32$)	.7400 ($n = 30$)	.0256
Year 2	.8000 ($n = 35$)	.8104 ($n = 67$)	.0104
Year 3	.9632 ($n = 38$)	.9860 ($n = 50$)	.0228

Note. MI = mean improvement.

more evenly distributed, with 59% of the responses being in agreement with the positive statement and 43% being in agreement with the negative statement. Overall, then, the children appeared to exhibit positive attitudes toward the components of the Academic Coaching Program during the 1997–1998 academic year.

During the 1998–1999 academic year, 43 of the 50 children participating in the Academic Coaching Program responded to the attitude survey. Again, their overall attitudes were positive. Seventy-two percent of the responses were in agreement with positive statements pertaining to Curriculum and Instruction, whereas 41% of the responses were in agreement with negative statements pertaining to this category. Seventy-nine percent of the responses were in agreement with positive statements about Teacher (Coach) Characteristics, whereas 33% were in agreement with the only negative statement pertaining to this category. Forty-eight percent of the responses were in agreement with positive statements pertaining to Student Characteristics, whereas 25% were in agreement with negative statements pertaining to Student Characteristics. Similar to the previous year, 60% of the responses were in agreement with the positive statement pertaining the Physical Setting in which the tutoring took place, whereas 37% were in agreement with the negative statement.

Figure 1 summarizes the percentages of positive and negative statements with which students agreed for each of 2 years of the Academic Coaching Program during which the survey was administered. The graph shows percentages of both positive and negative responses for each of the four categories of statements included on the Student Attitude Scale—the curriculum and instruction, the tutors, the students themselves, and the setting. The graph indicates consistent patterns of high percentages of agreement with positive statements about all four elements of the program. It also indicates consistent patterns of lower percentages of agreement with the negative statements included in the survey, thus revealing overall positive attitudes toward the Academic Coaching Program.

In addition, open-ended questions were added to the survey and indicated that 73% of the students would recommend the Academic Coaching Program to their friends. Many stated that they believed that the program helped them to understand their work better and that there was value to the program. Ten percent of the students would not recommend the Academic Coaching Program due to lack of in-

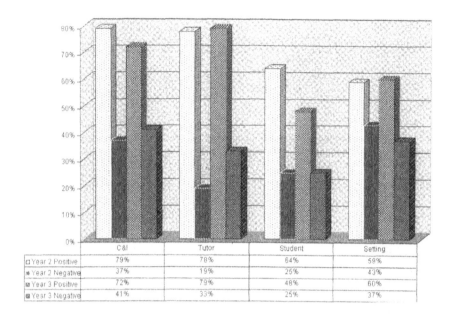

	C&I	Tutor	Student	Setting
▢ Year 2 Positive	79%	78%	64%	59%
▨ Year 2 Negative	37%	19%	25%	43%
▨ Year 3 Positive	72%	79%	48%	60%
▨ Year 3 Negative	41%	33%	25%	37%

FIGURE 1   Student attitude scale for years 2 and 3. C&I = Curriculum and Instruction.

crease in their grades and test scores. Students expressed a variety of reasons for liking the Academic Coaching Program. They most frequently stated that having fun while learning and the coach taking time with a student when she or he needed additional help in understanding material were important to them. One student stated, "What I like about tutoring is that you get a lot done there and you have lots of fun doing it." Another wrote, "I like being able to vote my opinion without being criticized." A third stated, "I like that my tutor really helps me with what I have trouble with. We have these flip cards and they really help you with things you don't know." And finally, one wrote, "I like how I get treated."

Giving students an opportunity to express what they disliked about the Academic Coaching Program yielded interesting results as well. Sixty-one percent of the students stated that there was nothing about the program they disliked. This suggests a high level of satisfaction. The remaining 39% indicated that their major concerns centered on curriculum issues. During the second semester, coaches focused on both reading and math. Many students, however, felt that math was not stressed enough. The Academic Coaching Program had a set curriculum that often did not leave time to work with students independently on problems.

One student wrote, "I dislike the fact we don't do enough math. I also dislike the fact that we get out at 2:45 (15 min later than the rest of the student body). I also dislike that they don't ever ask what we are having problems with."

CONCLUSIONS

Overall, the Academic Coaching Program yielded positive attitudes toward the components of the program from the at-risk students participating in it. It also yielded statistically significant grade equivalency gains from year to year in both reading and math scores for those at-risk students participating in the program. The program did not yield statistically significant differences in either reading or math between the grade equivalency gains of those participating in the program and those at the same grade level not participating in the program. During Years 1 and 2 of the program, however, participants in the program did outperform, in terms of grade equivalency gains, those not participating in the program in reading both years and in math during the 1st year.

That there were no statistically significant differences in grade equivalency gains on the Iowa Test of Basic Skills between the group participating in the Academic Coaching Program and those not participating in it is not surprising. The children not participating in the program were, for the most part, those who were determined not to need assistance in reading and math beyond the regular school program. This determination was based on prior achievement and teacher recommendation. One would, however, expect that the group not participating in the program would significantly out-gain the children deemed in need of additional assistance such as that provided by the Academic Coaching Program. Data to determine exact expected gains of either group were unavailable. What is particularly positive about the results is that the children who participated in the program made statistically significant gains that would not have been expected without additional assistance beyond the school's regular instructional program during all 3 years of the program. An unexpected result is that students participating in the Academic Coaching Program out-gained (even though not statistically significantly) those deemed not in need of assistance in both reading and math during the 1st year of the program and in reading during the 2nd year of the program.

A second somewhat unexpected result is that, although the mean gains in math increased from Year 1 (.7656) to Year 2 (.8000) to Year 3 (.9632) for those participating in the program, the mean gains in reading increased from Year 1 (.9450) to Year 2 (.9514) but not to Year 3 (.6564). One viable explanation for this is that methods and materials used to coach the students in math during all 3 years were designed specifically to target areas tested by the Iowa Test of Basic Skills. In reading, methods and materials used during Years 1 and 2 were specifically designed to enhance the children's test-taking competency, whereas, in Year 3, the Reciprocal Teaching methodology and selections chosen for it neither addressed specifically areas targeted by the Iowa Test of Basic Skills nor enhanced the children's test-taking competency. Rather, they were used to enhance the children's discussions during the Socratic seminars held each week in their regular classes.

Though the differences in improvement between the children in the program were not greater than those not in the program in math during the 2nd year of the program nor in either reading or math during the 3rd year of the program, they are certainly important to educators working with the children deemed to be most at risk in a school population in which approximately 96% of the children are at risk due to socioeconomic factors. This evaluation of the Academic Coaching Program, therefore, shows it to be effective at enhancing the education of this population of children. At a time when the successes of American schools and their students are being measured primarily by scores on standardized tests, this evaluation emphasizes the importance of adequately preparing children to take the tests. It also emphasizes the potential sacrifices of other important academic skills—particularly higher order thinking skills not measured by standardized tests—when focusing primarily on students' gains on those tests.

ACKNOWLEDGMENTS

The program and evaluation on which this article are based were supported by grants from the Chicago Public School's *10,000 Tutors* initiative. The content does not necessarily reflect the views of the Chicago Public Schools or any other agency of the City of Chicago. An earlier version of this article was presented at the Sixteenth International Congress for School Effectiveness and Improvement in Sydney, Australia in January 2003.

REFERENCES

Adler, M. J. (1982). *The Paideia proposal: An educational manifesto.* New York: Macmillan.
Adler, M. J. (1983). *Paideia problems and possibilities: A consideration of questions raised by The Paideia proposal.* New York: Macmillan.
Adler, M. J. (1984). *The Paideia program: An educational syllabus.* New York: Macmillan.
Balfanz, R., Ruby, A., & Mac Iver, D. (2002). Essential components and next steps for comprehensive whole-school reform in high poverty middle schools. In S. Stringfield & D. Land (Eds.), *Educating at-risk students* (pp. 128–147). Chicago: University of Chicago Press.
Cobb, J. B. (1998). The social contexts of tutoring: Mentoring the older at-risk student. *Reading Horizons, 39,* 49–75.
Estes, T. (n.d.). *Estes attitude scale.* Charlottesville, VA: Virginia Research Associates Ltd.
Fitzgerald, J. (2001). Can minimally trained college student volunteers help young at-risk children to read better? *Reading Research Quarterly, 36,* 28–47.
Heins, E. D., Perry, A., & Piechura-Couture, K. (1999). Stetson reads: An after-school tutorial program for at-risk students. *Reading Improvement, 36,* 116–121.
Palincsar, A. S., & Brown, A. L. (1984). Reciprocal teaching of comprehension fostering and comprehension monitoring activities. *Cognition and Instruction, 2,* 117–175.
Schiller, D., Giroux, D., Gozan, D., & Thomas, C. (Developers). (1991–2002). *Countdown* [Television series]. Chicago: Cable Access Channel.

Shumow, L. (2001). *Academic effects of after-school programs.* Champaign, IL ERIC Clearinghouse on Elementary and Early Childhood Education. (ERIC Document No. ED458010).

Slavin, R. E. (2002). *Educational psychology: Theory and practice* (7th ed). Boston: Allyn and Bacon.

Tingley, J. (2001). Volunteer programs: When good intentions are not enough. *Education Leadership, 68,* 53–55.

Van Doren, C. (1984). Mathematics. In M. J. Adler (Ed.), *The Paideia program: An educational syllabus* (pp. 71–85). New York: Macmillan.

Van Doren, G. (1984). English Language and Literature. In M. J. Adler (Ed.), *The Paideia program: An educational syllabus* (pp. 59–70). New York: Macmillan.

Wasik, B. A. (1997). Volunteer tutoring programs: Do we know what works? *Phi Delta Kappan, 79,* 283–287.

Wasik, B. A., & Slavin, R. E. (1993). Preventing early reading failure with one-to-one tutoring: A review of five programs. *Reading Research Quarterly, 28,* 178–200.

APPENDIX
Tutoring Attitude Scale

Directions: This is a scale to measure how you feel about the tutoring program in your school. Below you will read some statements about tutoring. Please rate each sentence on this scale:

A will mean "I agree."
? will mean "I don't know."
D will mean "I disagree."

A ___ ? ___ D ___   1. Math is easy to learn when we work in tutoring groups.

A ___ ? ___ D ___   2. Tutors confuse students because they don't explain things the same way that teachers do.

A ___ ? ___ D ___   3. It is hard to understand math when students work with a tutor in small groups.

A ___ ? ___ D ___   4. It is enjoyable to talk about stories with classmates in tutoring groups.

A ___ ? ___ D ___   5. Solving math problems with string, crayons, and other materials is helpful in learning math.

A ___ ? ___ D ___   6. Reading is an activity that is best done alone in a quiet place.

A ___ ? ___ D ___   7. Tutors help students learn better by guiding students through the material at a slower pace than teachers.

A ___ ? ___ D ___   8. To learn math, students must complete many worksheets of problems.

A ___ ? ___ D ___   9. Tutors are like older friends that can help a student learn.

A ___ ? ___ D ___   10. Most students spend their tutoring time playing instead of working.

A ___ ? ___ D ___   11. Tutors are like teachers who can help students learn.

A ___ ? ___ D ___   12. Sometimes it is easier to understand a reading assignment when one or two classmates work together in tutoring groups.

A ___ ? ___ D ___   13. In tutoring sessions it is alright to make mistakes.

A ___ ? ___ D ___   14. The cafeteria is a good place for tutoring because the groups can all fit but still have separate areas to meet.

A ___ ? ___ D ___   15. Students who do not go to tutoring make fun of students who attend.

A ___ ? ___ D ___   16. The work done in tutoring is similar to the work done in class.

A ___ ? ___ D ___   17. Tutoring groups should meet in separate rooms.

A ___ ? ___ D ___   18. Students who attend tutoring are more likely to do better on IGAP and IOWA tests than they would have without tutoring.

A ___ ? ___ D ___   19. Students who attend tutoring miss important class activities.

(continued)

APPENDIX *(Continued)*

A ___ ? ___ D ___   20. It is hard to figure out how the activities done in tutoring are related to what is done in class.

A ___ ? ___ D ___   21. Many students at school wish they could be in tutoring.

A ___ ? ___ D ___   22. Students would do better to skip tutoring and stay in class.

A ___ ? ___ D ___   23. In tutoring, other students in the group make fun of the students who don't know the answers.

A ___ ? ___ D ___   24. Students who don't go to tutoring would like to be able to go.

A ___ ? ___ D ___   25. Reading activities done in tutoring help students read better.

26. In tutoring, students spend most of their time working.

Please answer the following questions as thoughtfully as you can. Your answers will remain confidential. For those of you who have attended more than one semester, be sure to consider all the semesters in the program.

Grade _____ Sex _____

1. How many semesters have you attended the Loyola Tutoring Program?

2. What do you like about the tutoring program? What activities taught you the most?

3. What do you dislike about the tutoring program? What activities taught you the least?

4. Describe your most positive memorable experience in tutoring.

5. Describe your most negative memorable experience in tutoring.

6. Would you recommend this program to your friends? Why or why not?

JOURNAL OF EDUCATION FOR STUDENTS PLACED AT RISK, *10*(2), 225–228

BOOK REVIEW

No Child Left Behind? The Politics and Practice of School Accountability.
Edited by Paul E. Peterson and Martin R. West, Washington, DC: Brookings
Institution Press, 2003, 320 pages, $22.95 (softcover), $52.95 (hardcover).

Shelley H. Billig
RMC Research Corporation, Denver

As a result of the experience of many states like Texas and North Carolina, educators in the year 2000 were energized by the standards movement; putting standards into place seemed to be the best strategy for becoming more competitive internationally. Having standards meant being clear on what was expected for all students in any school for all subject matters. Standards specified expectations for student achievement, brought consistency and coherence to the educational system, and promoted equity by having the same expectations for all students.

Having content and performance standards, however, was only a first step. The next decision was how standards could drive change so that all students would meet standards. Prior to 2000, two strands of thought were in place: catalyze change through a strong accountability system that featured rewards and consequences or nurture change through the provision of professional development. Early studies of progress made in Texas and North Carolina showed that accountability systems with consequences were the faster route to change, and one that resonated with more policymakers. Thus, in 2001, the No Child Left Behind (NCLB) Act was passed with bipartisan support, and educators were given 12 years to reach the "dream" of having all children master the standards with "no child left behind."

The maelstrom that followed was predictable. The educational endeavor is not an easy one, and not like a mechanistic process for producing widgets to some specifications set by a monitoring agency. Though the idea of standards was still generally attractive in the aftermath of the passage of NCLB, the actual measurement of performance to determine whether students were meeting standards was subject to widespread disagreement. If consequences were to be attached to perfor-

Requests for reprints should be sent to Shelley H. Billig, RMC Research Corporation, Writer Square, Suite 540, 1512 Larimer Street, Denver, CO 80202. E-mail: billig@rmcdenver.com

mance, educators wanted the measurements to be fair and accurate. Educators' jobs and students' future lives were at stake.

No Child Left Behind? The Politics and Practice of School Accountability provides an array of analyses of the politics, practice, and promise of accountability. The book is fascinating because it provides an in-depth examination of multiple facets of the legislation, the ways in which the policies are being implemented, and the early evidence of success and failure of various components of the law. Many of the authors do not take a neutral stance, but rather have a point of view that is strongly influenced by their own political philosophies. Several authors, including West, Peterson, and Rudalevige, are not particularly appreciative of teachers or teacher unions. Other authors, including Moe and Hochschild, are skeptical of the motives behind the law.

The essays in this book on the politics of accountability provide insights with a strong conservative bent. The political analyses are thoughtful, whether the reader agrees or disagrees. Authors provide evidence to support their arguments. However, some readers may find that the evidence can be interpreted in multiple ways; they may reach conclusions other than those provided within the chapters. For example, several of the analyses purport that teachers' unions and teachers themselves have been the chief stumbling block to successful implementation of the law because they have "softened the strategies" (organizational control mechanisms) within NCLB that are most likely to make a difference. In the first few essays, this point of view is strongly promoted and West and Peterson and Rudalevige and Hess name the individuals who were responsible for many of these ideas and compromises. Several of these authors spare no verbiage in placing blame on teachers and their union representatives for the difficulties that have ensued during the first year of NCLB implementation.

The political consequences of enacting NCLB are explained in detail in several of the chapters. Hanushek and Raymond, for example, detail the tensions experienced by politicians who endorse the tenets of NCLB but do not want to enforce strong coercive consequences because those actions may lead to educator unrest, public outcry, and problems with teacher retention in schools, all of which influence those politicians' chances of re-election. By selecting certain standards, other content areas are ignored; by setting certain levels of mastery, some percentages of students and schools are destined to be identified for improvement; and by setting consequences, some groups are likely to be targeted. Each of these choices engenders opposition, and as consequences become more severe, the opposition becomes more intense. This type of opposition frequently leads to mobilization of groups that have similar feelings about the law, and as more groups mobilize to oppose the law, compromises are more likely to occur and the theory behind the law is called into question. This type of force field analysis allows the reader to become more acutely aware of the many layers of impact, both intended and unintended, that have occurred since the passage of NCLB.

Several of the early chapters also discuss the effects of political compromise in the way that the law was constructed. The authors conclude that the compromises are such that states simply cannot be successful in reaching the lofty aims embodied in the law. These essays reveal certain limitations of the law, and show the ways in which some states have lowered standards, postponed consequences, and held educators accountable without holding students accountable. Nearly half of the authors in the book believe that the compromises that were necessary to pass the law will be its undoing.

Many of the chapters address the flaws in the accountability system embedded in NCLB. Accountability under NCLB is based on cross-sectional analysis, where grade-level outcomes are compared to the same grade-level outcomes from the preceding year. This type of accountability increases pressure to improve quality at that grade level, but brings to the fore the many measurement errors that occur by comparing different populations of students each year. Some of the more sophisticated analyses presented in the book compare accountability systems based on cross-sectional versus longitudinal analysis (the same students over time) and show the challenges associated with each. These chapters generally show the benefits of longitudinal analysis over cross-sectional analysis.

Another set of analyses by Kane and Staiger shows unintended consequences of disaggregating by subgroup categories such as race or socioeconomic status. These analyses show that schools with more diversity are more likely to be identified for improvement based on the diversity factor alone. Data are presented at the student, school, district, and state level, and analyzed to show likely consequences for accountability at each level given the current profile of achievement. Big cities will bear the burden of this portion of the law, according to chapters by Hanushek and Raymond, Bryk, and Jacob, because it is inevitable that urban schools will be identified for corrective actions. Loveless, Betts, and Danenberg also discuss the issues associated with charter schools, along with the unique problems in accountability that are faced by those in rural settings.

Data and experiences from several states and cities are examined in detail. For example, the Chicago experience with implementing the NCLB provisions is investigated by Bryk and Jacobs, who analyze policies and test scores. Bryk notes that the law galvanized public attention on education, but that outcomes thus far have been modest at best. Bryk also points out the serious deficiencies in the measurement system that is in use. Jacobs, also writing about the Chicago experience, highlights the fact that gains have been made over time, in the aggregate, particularly in students' mastery of basic mathematics skills and reading. However, he warns that results may not be generalizable because it is not yet clear whether the results can be attributed to change in instructional practice.

The final essay in the book reflects an international perspective and argues strongly for the effectiveness of central exams in promoting increases in student achievement. Analysis of data from the Third International Mathematics and Science Studies (TIMSS) from 1995 and 1999 bolsters the argument that central examination systems do not necessarily dictate instructional design, but rather can work well with autonomous local systems so that classroom teachers in any state can flexibly apply techniques as long as they address the subject matter to be mastered. Wofsmann provides evidence to show the long-term positive effects of the exams.

No Child Left Behind? The Politics and Practice of School Accountability illuminates the system-level issues and tensions that have surfaced over the past few years and will appeal strongly to those who enjoy deconstructing educational policies and examining implications in detail. More general audiences are less likely to be captivated by this book because it is so detailed, sometimes redundant, and aimed toward those who can appreciate sophisticated analyses of both political and measurement systems.

The bottom line, however, is that this book has many thought-provoking essays that are likely to form the basis of policy considerations for the future. The authors elucidate the issues well and provide some of the evidence needed to understand how and why this legislation came to be, the ways in which the policies are playing out, and the consequences of implementation.

JOURNAL OF EDUCATION FOR STUDENTS PLACED AT RISK, *10*(2), 229–231

BOOK REVIEW

Research Informing Policy: *Teacher Quality: Understanding the Effectiveness of Teacher Attributes.* Jennifer King Rice, Washington, DC: Economic Policy Institute, 2003, 64 pages, $11.50 (softcover).

Robert J. Stevens
Department of Educational Psychology
The Pennsylvania State University

Teacher Quality: Understanding the Effectiveness of Teacher Attributes is an interesting attempt by Jennifer King Rice to relate educational research to educational policy and practice. This is an important endeavor. With the increase in legislative initiatives in education that mandate both policy and practice, Rice is to be commended for this straightforward attempt to look at existing research that addresses specific policy-related issues. In this short text, Rice focuses her examination of this research on five areas: teacher experience, teacher preparation and degree, teacher certification, teacher coursework, and teacher test scores. Each of these variables, or "teacher attributes" as Rice calls them, are relevant to policy discussions at the federal, state, and local levels in terms of who can teach, how much they get paid, and how we prepare future teachers.

In the first chapter of the book, Rice establishes the importance of looking at the topic of teacher characteristics in terms of social, economic, and historical contexts. Socially, there is little question that teachers have a large impact on the students they teach, and that high-quality teachers play important roles in the lives of children and the community they serve. Rice also makes a strong case economically for the importance of schools investing in high-quality teachers. She cites teachers' salaries as the largest single budget item for most school districts. Thus schools must find adequate selection processes to identify high-quality teachers so that districts can spend their resources wisely. In the first chapter, Rice also establishes a research context for this work: She attempts to delineate the previous uses of this type of review methodology. By doing so, she establishes the groundwork for her discussion of her methodology in chapter 2.

Requests for reprints should be sent to Robert J. Stevens, Educational Psychology, 202 Cedar Building, The Pennsylvania State University, University Park, PA 16802. E-mail: rjs15@psu.edu

Chapter 2 describes Rice's methodology, how she selected the studies to include in the review, and how she interpreted the studies in a way to make sense of them. She acknowledges that there are important differences in the studies she has used, including their methodological rigor and the types of outcome variables they use. Rice is careful to suggest to the reader that more rigorous studies may yield more dependable results. Yet the author emphasizes that her goal is to provide a more inclusive look at the research on teacher quality, hence her inclusion of a broad variety of research in the belief that it will provide the readers with more contextual information about teacher quality variables. As she states, "the goal is not to boil down studies of quantitative summaries of what matters, but rather to synthesize the literature in a way that brings qualitative meaning to the array of studies that have been conducted" (p. 10). This is an admirable goal if one is careful to differentiate the studies based on their methodological rigor and the types of outcome measures used.

In the third chapter, Rice provides a synthesis of the research on the attributes of teacher experience, teacher preparation and degree, teacher certification, teacher coursework, and teacher test scores. Each section provides an interesting discussion of the research related to that attribute. Rice found that some areas have adequate research (e.g., teacher coursework), whereas others seem, at least to this reader, to have poorly designed research that does not control for a variety of mitigating variables (e.g., teacher preparation programs).

The last chapter offers the author's summary of the research with some implications of her findings for policy issues that face schools and legislatures. Perhaps the most notable and most important conclusion that Rice offers is the strong evidence in support of pedagogical coursework in teacher preparation programs. Courses that teach teachers how to teach seem to contribute to teacher effectiveness at all grade levels. This finding is notable given that many state legislative initiatives push teachers to have bachelor's degrees in specific subject matters and de-emphasize pedagogical training. From her reading of the literature, Rice also concludes that teacher content area certification is related to teaching efficacy only in high school mathematics. These two conclusions suggest that training in specific content areas may not be as important for teacher efficacy as is training in pedagogical areas like student learning and motivation and classroom management. Although one suspects that the existing research does not suggest that, no preparation in the content area is required. Instead it is likely that there is a minimal level of training that is necessary, and that teachers are not likely to volunteer to teach content they are totally unprepared to teach.

Another attribute for which Rice was able to find fairly conclusive research related teacher test scores to student performance. Though teaching exams like the National Teacher Examination were found to have mixed results in the research, Rice found that literacy examinations did yield positive effects on student achievement, particularly for at-risk students.

On other attributes, Rice had difficulty making firm conclusions based on research that was either inconclusive or contradictory. Rice did find that teacher experience does improve student achievement, particularly for the first 3 years; this is a conclusion that has been educational "common knowledge" for years, and one worth delineating with the solid empirical data provided. Beyond 3 years, there seem to be few significant effects except for another positive bump at 14 years. This is a curious finding, and one that Rice does little to explicate. For the attribute of teacher preparation programs, the author concludes that there are mixed results, some inconclusive. There also seem to be no firm conclusions about emergency or alternative routes to certification.

This book clearly has important information for policymakers, like school superintendents, state superintendents, and legislators. The teacher attributes selected are pertinent, and, in many cases, Rice's conclusions are quite enlightening and run counter to conventional wisdom. At the very least, I recommend chapters 1 and 4 as required reading for individuals involved in teacher hiring or certification issues.

Unfortunately, I believe the book offers much less for other readers, especially educational researchers. The book lacks the methodological rigor of a meta-analysis and the measured reasoning of a classic review. Though the author notes the importance of methodological rigor in the studies, she does not differentiate the usefulness or impact of the study based on that rigor. She treats the conclusions of a study with good experimental design as equal to those from a study with much less methodological rigor, when more emphasis should go to the findings of the former. Similarly, Rice treats all quantitative outcome measures the same, when conceptually and empirically there are substantial differences. For example, a study that uses teacher's perceptions of their own preparation for teaching should not have the same impact as a study that measures the effects on student achievement. This type of mixing of apples and oranges throughout the review makes this text of very limited usefulness to educational researchers.

Generally this book offers an interesting discussion of the research on five teacher characteristics. This discussion is relevant and important for policymakers and those who implement policy. The information provided will support some notions we have long held in education, and hopefully some of the other findings will help us think more accurately about decision making for training, hiring, and rewarding teachers.

JOURNAL OF EDUCATION FOR STUDENTS PLACED AT RISK, *10*(2), 233–234

NOTES ON CONTRIBUTORS

CHRISTIANNA L. ALGER is an assistant professor in the School of Teacher Education at San Diego State University. Recent research interests have included resilience of at-risk students, teacher development, and professional development schools.

RUTH L. BASKERVILLE is the principal of Norman S. Weir Elementary School in Paterson, NJ.

SHELLEY H. BILLIG is Vice President of RMC Research Corporation and has conducted multiple studies of education reform initiatives and NCLB implementation.

FAY E. BROWN is an Associate Research Scientist at Yale Child Study Center and Director of Child and Adolescent Development for the School Development Program.

CHRISTINE L. EMMONS is an associate research scientist with the School Development Program, Yale University Child Study Center.

BRUCE M. FRAZEE is a professor of education at Trinity University and a clinical faculty member at Hawthorne Academy, San Antonio, TX.

FELICIA F. FRAZEE is a student of Education with a specialization in Special Education at Trinity University, San Antonio, TX.

ELDA E. MARTINEZ, a doctoral candidate in Educational Administration at Teachers College, Columbia University, is employed by the San Antonio Independent School District and is currently teaching special education courses at Trinity University.

DEBRA MENTZER is a National Board Certified teacher of seventh graders at Hawthorne Academy in San Antonio, TX. She has received several national awards for teaching and mentoring.

EDWARD T. MURRAY is an associate professor of Education and Director of Literacy Programs at Sacred Heart University.

PAMELA S. NESSELRODT is an associate professor in the Education Department at Dickinson College. Her research interests include school reform, program development and evaluation, teacher effectiveness and resilience, and improving the educational opportunities of children placed at risk.

TRICIA SHAUGHNESSY has been a primary grade teacher for 25 years. She enjoys teaching and learning with her students at Hawthorne Academy in San Antonio, TX.

ROBERT J. STEVENS is a professor of Educational Psychology and department head of the Educational and School Psychology and Special Education Department at the Pennsylvania State University. He does research in literacy and remediation of literacy problems, with a focus on students who are at risk of academic failure.

SAMUEL C. STRINGFIELD is the Academic Director of the Nystrand Center of Excellence in Education and a professor in the departments of Leadership, Foundations, and Human Resource Education and Teaching and Learning at the University of Louisville. He is the editor of the *Journal of Education for Students Placed At Risk* (*JESPAR*), author of over 100 articles, books, and chapters on teacher effectiveness and school reform, and the former vice-chair of the Board of Education of Baltimore City Public Schools.

KIRSTEN EWART SUNDELL, managing editor of *JESPAR*, is a senior research associate and adjunct assistant faculty member in the College of Education and Human Development at the University of Louisville. With Sam Stringfield, she is currently co-editing *The Search for Equity in Education: Experiences and Directions from Developing and Developed Countries* and co-authoring a book on the history of Baltimore City school reforms.

www.ingramcontent.com/pod-product-compliance
Ingram Content Group UK Ltd.
Pitfield, Milton Keynes, MK11 3LW, UK
UKHW020427010325
455677UK00029B/1043